M000274819

CC41
UTILITY
CLOTHING

The Label that Transformed British Fashion

MIKE BROWN

SABRESTORM

Designed and typeset by Philip Clucas MSIAD

Studio photographs Copyright © 2014 Ian Bayley

British Library Cataloguing in Publication Data

A catalogue record for this book is available from
the British Library

Published by Sabrestorm Publishing, 90 Lennard
Road, Dunton Green, Sevenoaks, Kent TN13 2UX

Website: www.sabrestorm.com
Email: books@sabrestorm.com

Printed in Singapore by Tien Wah Press

ISBN 978-1-78122-005-4

Contents

Utility 4

Background 6

A Standard Suit? 10

Rationing 16

The Utility Scheme 24

Concentration & Designation 38

Footwear 46

Utility in Operation 52
November 1941 to June 1942

Wot – No Turn-ups? 62

The Couturier Scheme 70

Utility Furs 76

Stockings 82

Foundation Garments 86

Utility in Operation 94
July 1942 to November 1945

Post-War Utility 102

The End of Utility 118

Acknowledgements 128

Utility

By the end of the Second World War, the word 'Utility' encompassed a wide range of goods, including clothes, footwear, furniture, pencils, cigarette lighters, textiles and crockery. It described affordable and well-made items, produced using as little labour and raw materials as possible. To achieve this, the Government took control of their design as well as the chain of production and supply.

Such control was achieved by the passage of sweeping legislation, and under the direction of a growing network of civil servants running a system based on complex regulations designed to cover every stage of production up to the point of sale.

This book documents and describe the evolution and development of the Utility Clothing scheme, using official records, biographies, newspaper reports and magazine articles of the period.

AUNTIE'S UTILITY'S
COME DOWN TO ME!

RIGHT Utility covered shoes as well as clothing.

OPPOSITE PAGE A beautiful utility dress. The two plain coloured cloths that make it up mean that no material is wasted in matching up pieces.
LEFT Close-up of its 'CC41' utility label.

Background

During the First World War modern mechanised warfare consumed vast quantities of raw materials, most of which had to be imported into the United Kingdom. Naval blockades, made all the more effective by the advent of the submarine, sought to strangle such imports. The war effort took priority with regard to the available resources with the result that civilians suffered shortages. In Britain, the Government's laissez-faire philosophy meant that

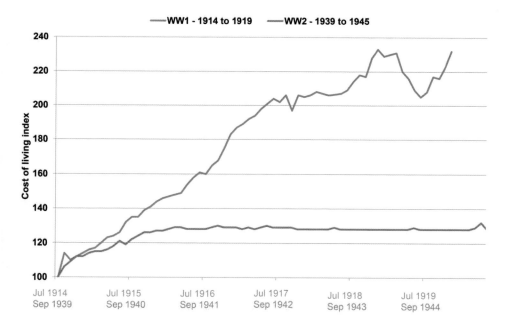

MONTHLY RISE IN THE COST OF LIVING INDEX JULY 1914–19 AND SEPTEMBER 1939–45

The graph clearly shows that during both conflicts the cost of living rose sharply in the first few months of war. However, after five or six months the line representing the First World War continues its steep increase, whereas the Second World War line begins to flatten off, becoming virtually stable within 18 months.

OPPOSITE PAGE Woman's three-quarter length 'super-utility' coat. It's shortness meant a large saving in material, the tie belt saved on metal for the buckle, and the pouch pockets saved on labour.

the laws of supply and demand were allowed to accommodate such shortages through price rises – between 1914 and 1918 the cost of living index rose by a massive 250 per cent. By 1918 this had created serious problems in providing food and clothing for a growing number of the population, forcing the government to introduce food rationing.

The inter-war years saw growing public criticism of a system under which profiteers had earned not only vast fortunes, but also been granted honours, while the poor were left to suffer. By 1939 few believed that the vagaries of the market should be allowed to have such a profound effect on civilian life in Britain. The Prices of Goods Act,

The symbol of the Board of Trade, a body that was tasked with introducing the Utility clothing scheme.

which became law in mid-November 1939, gave the Board of Trade – a vast Government department that oversaw all aspects of industry except food and munitions – the power to fix maximum prices for any items deemed essential. On 1 January 1940 the Board set maximum prices for a raft of items including clothes and shoes.

Food rationing was also introduced. These steps to protect civilians from the long-term privations of war were described as 'war socialism' by Winston Churchill, among others, who understood that a modern war could only be won

To prevent waste a new Government order prohibits the free distribution of our catalogues, therefore to comply, this and future issues will be charged 1d. and debited to your account.

Also the quantity being strictly limited to one-fifth, we are only able to send to special regular customers, hoping you will make the most possible use by showing it to your friends and retaining it as long as possible for reference.

The elimination of waste became a national priority.

through centralised control of industry and the economy. As Lord Woolton, a Conservative peer and Minister of Food from 1940 to 1943, later wrote: 'We arrived at a position in which, in time of war, the practices that would be normal under a socialist state seemed to be the only practical safeguards for the country.'

OPPOSITE PAGE A typical woman's suit in super-utility. Saving in labour and material is achieved by it being single-breasted, having a maximum of three buttons, and an absolute minimum of pleats in the skirt – yet the design keeps it stylish.

A Standard Suit?

As the First World War dragged on, daily life became a question of who could hold out longest, as raw materials were devoured by the military machine, leaving little for civilians.

In 1917 the Government, responding to shortages, planned to manufacture 'Standard Cloth' for civilian use. In November it was announced that the scheme would provide made-up garments. In June 1918, at an exhibition of this clothing, the **Bradford Weekly Telegraph** reported the Postmaster General as saying '*...something like 70% of the wool coming into the country was being used for official purposes alone...The small amount of cloth available for civilian purposes had led to prices being forced up to an unprecedented level, so much so that a good many people were getting restless and war weary, but now that the Government had taken control of things which were indispensable there was a much better feeling. The control of articles of food had been followed by the introduction of the standard boot, and now they were to have standard cloth, so that people could be supplied with serviceable garments at reasonable prices.*'

TO DRESS EXTRAVAGANTLY IN WAR TIME IS WORSE THAN BAD FORM IT IS UNPATRIOTIC

A First World War poster – saving money and raw materials by not buying unnecessarily was recognised as a patriotic sacrifice.

'Standard' suits, jackets and trousers for men and boys were produced, as well as boots, hosiery and underwear for women and children, and a 'National Standard dress' for women and girls.

OPPOSITE PAGE Men's super-utility suit. Just like the women's suit on page 9, this man's version saves both material and labour by being single-breasted, with a maximum of three buttons – however, the question of turn-ups and waistcoats would prove contentious.

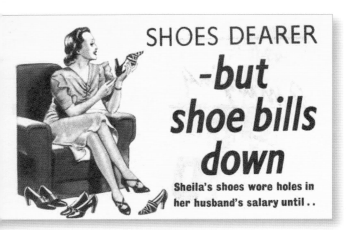

SHOES DEARER
-but
shoe bills
down

Sheila's shoes wore holes in
her husband's salary until..

An advertisement for stick-on soles
from December 1939, demonstrating
the rising cost of footwear.

There were problems. Manufacturers claimed that, due to wage rises and the fixed price, they made a loss on the suits, although prices were raised several times. Some standard cloth was requisitioned for military use, and the women's dress was universally condemned. The **Daily Mirror** in October 1941 told readers, *'If you were at school round about 1918 you may remember how your navy blue tunic faded to a dim greyish purple after a few weeks' wear. Or how your top-coat ravelled out in little bits before you had really begun to get used to the colour. Your mother will certainly remember how she had to shop around for underwear and shoes and the prices she had to pay for them.'*

In June 1940 **The Times** commented, *'The last scheme for supplying standard clothing failed because it did not provide sufficient profit, although the price of a standard suit was double what a suit of the very best cloth cost before the war'*. Later, in their book, **British War Economy**, the historians W. K. Hancock and M. M. Gowing argued that the scheme's fundamental weakness was that there was no compulsion to enforce it; manufacturers and distributors could opt out, and since the business was comparatively unprofitable, many did. **The Times** quoted an 'authority' who declared that *'the last scheme fell through because the distributors displayed no enthusiasm for it, the fixed profit not being enough for them. Unless the Government take over all the machinery and control the price of the article from the raw material onwards, and compel the manufacturers to make quantities of standard cloth, the scheme would fail.'*

About the only thing that's come down since the war!

A First World War postcard reflects on price rises. The caption says it all.

When war broke out in September 1939 these ideas were not forgotten. When food rationing was introduced in January 1940, the press speculated that other measures would soon follow. The **Daily Express** warned that *'Rationing in silk stockings and many other women's "etceteras", in household utensils, and even "standard suits" for men may have to be introduced as part of an immediate new "all-out" war effort.'*

On 10 September, the **Daily Mail** declared, *'No "Pool" suits yet'*. The **Daily Mirror** predicted that *'Standard suits will be elegant, well cut and low in cost. The price will be fixed at £3 10s. There will be a wide range of patterns. There is no need to fear that your "ration suit" will look like a roadman's jacket and a pair of dungarees.'*

In a letter to the **Hull Daily Mail**, the President of the local Master Tailors wrote: *'To us, it seems ridiculous that everyone will have to wear a standard suit, and I think it would be most unfair to ask the public to have just one mediocre type of suit without a*

Another postcard from the First World War era. In June 1918 the Bishop of Stepney had observed that *'The really fashionable clothes today are clothes that have been mended.'*

TO DRESS EXTRAVAGANTLY IS BAD FORM AND UNPATRIOTIC

In the fashion at last!

LEFT Utility jacket, trousers, and shirt. The jacket has no breast pocket, nor does the shirt, a very utility feature.

choice of pattern.' A month later Parliament was told that the controlled price of wool was approximately 20 per cent above pre-war levels, whereas the uncontrolled prices of yarns and cloths were 60 to 100 per cent above pre-war rates.

The first focus of what would become the Utility scheme was furniture. Wood shortages drove up prices dramatically in the early months of the war. In response the government proposed to ban construction of all but specified 'standard' furniture that was to be plain and functional. Also furnishing fabrics featuring bold patterns that needed large repeats were deemed wasteful. Small patterns meant less waste, and well-made cloth would last longer. These ideas applied equally to clothing fabrics.

In March 1940 the Minister of Supply, Edward Leslie Burgin, was asked if the Government intended to standardise woollen cloths, and if he would introduce a scheme for pooling them. Pooling, as in 'pool petrol' or 'national butter', was a system whereby all imports of a product were consolidated and sold without brand names. Burgin replied that the Government was considering the production of woollen cloths at standard prices, although any arrangement could not come into operation for some time. Two weeks later he gave a similar answer when asked about a scheme for standard footwear.

I'm all austerity these days !

In April Burgin was asked if the issue of standard suits was still under consideration; he replied that no decision had yet been reached. On the same day footwear manufacturers told the government that the introduction of a standard shoe at that time would be premature.

A Second World War postcard – notice the first clothing ration card (issued in Autumn 1942) in the bottom corner.

On 5 March newspapers reported that the quota of civilian cloth to tailors was being cut by half; there would be fewer patterns to choose from and a standard suit might have to be introduced. On 21 March the Board of Trade introduced the first of several 'Making of Civilian Clothing [Restriction] Orders', commonly known as the Austerity Regulations. These limited the amount and types of material, buttons and trimmings that manufacturers, commercial dressmakers and tailors could use.

ABOVE Boy's utility cap. Adults' hats were never made part of the scheme, as there were far too many variations in style, but children's caps and bonnets were included.

During that month, while speaking on the BBC, Hugh Dalton (Minister of Economic Warfare) referred to 'standard' clothing. At the same time, the Economic Policy Committee recommended to the War Cabinet that the Government should buy 'standard cloth' for men's suits and sell it to makers-up, and that there should also be standard boots and shoes, with price margins fixed at each stage. The War Cabinet approved the scheme in principle, desiring it to be in operation by October. In fact, the idea would remain just a notion until events overtook it in mid-1941.

In April 1940 the Chancellor of the Exchequer, Sir Kingsley Wood, announced that, in order to reduce demand and stabilise prices, he was introducing purchase tax, to come into effect on 21 October. **The Times** described it as '*the one great new instrument for raising revenue which this war has produced*'.

In July 1941, Captain Charles Waterhouse, Parliamentary Secretary to the Board of Trade, informed Parliament that '*there is no evidence to show that the introduction of standard clothing is either necessary or desirable. My Right Hon. Friend recently appointed Mr. Metford Watkins as Director General of Civilian Clothing, to deal with questions arising on the supply and distribution and to make what arrangements are necessary to secure that adequate supplies of clothing, and in particular working-class clothing, are available for the population.*'

Rationing

At the beginning of May 1940, British forces in Norway were evacuated following a campaign that had been dogged by a lack of modern equipment, especially aircraft. On 8 May Prime Minister Neville Chamberlain asked the opposition to join him in a coalition, but they refused; there was a widespread feeling that he was an unsatisfactory war leader. There followed a two-day debate in which he faced criticism not only from the opposition, but also a substantial revolt within his own party. He resigned on 10 May, and was replaced by Winston Churchill, who formed a coalition government.

It was clear from the start that Churchill's overriding concern was the conduct of the war. In his first speech to parliament as Prime Minister, he said, *'You ask what is our policy, I would say it is to wage war by sea, land and air with all our might…you ask what is our aim, I can answer in one word: victory.'* His choice of cabinet reflected this. Ernest Bevin, General Secretary of the TGWU (Transport and General Workers' Union), became Minister of Labour and National Service, while the Labour stalwart Herbert Morrison replaced Burgin as Minister of Supply, and shortly afterwards was appointed Home Secretary. Even the Conservative Chancellor, Sir Kingsley Wood, appointed the left-leaning economist Maynard Keynes as Treasury adviser.

GOD didn't know when he made us to grow - there'd be coupons!

Rationing was tight, especially for children who, as the postcard shows, rapidly grew out of their clothes. For that reason, they were given extra coupons.

OPPOSITE PAGE Children's clothes, from the smallest baby clothes, were covered by the utility scheme, as with this baby's frock, and boy's buster-suit shirt. The dress is early; later even the small amount of embroidery of the two red lines would not be allowed.

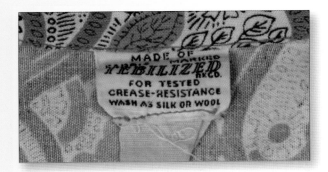

LEFT AND RIGHT Utility shirt-dress, with tie belt. Many early pieces had, like this, a makers label, and a separate, printed utility label, many of which, as with this example, quickly faded with washing, and are very difficult to read.

The huge demands on imports imposed by the armed services, war industries and civilian requirements could not possibly be met. The first stage of solving the problem was to differentiate between goods that were deemed necessary, and 'luxuries'. All ships had to carry at least a minimum of the former, and were only allowed a small quota of the latter.

Next it was established how much each of the three sectors – the services, munitions and civil use – really needed, and from this raw materials were allocated. Obviously supplies of raw materials available to be made into clothing or footwear for civilian use fell sharply. To avoid a free-for-all, whereby clothing manufacturers would scrabble to snap up as much raw material as possible, leading to a bidding war and inevitable price rises, the Government introduced LIMOSOs (Limitation of Supply Orders). These set a maximum amount that manufacturers could produce, based on a percentage of what they had produced in a given pre-war period (usually April–

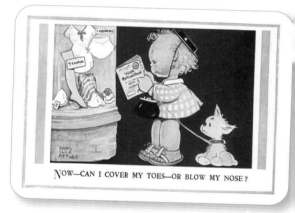

A postcard by the illustrator Mabel Lucie Attwell – clothing rationing left the consumer facing some hard choices.

September 1939), and on an assessment of how essential the goods were. In the case of clothing, the first LIMOSO of April 1940 dictated a 25 per cent cut in cotton and rayon, and a massive 75 per cent cut in linen.

At first this drop in supply was not noticeable; demand fell off, as thousands were called-up for military service, and clothing reserves covered the shortfall. The industry had little trouble producing 500 million yards of blackout cloth in the first

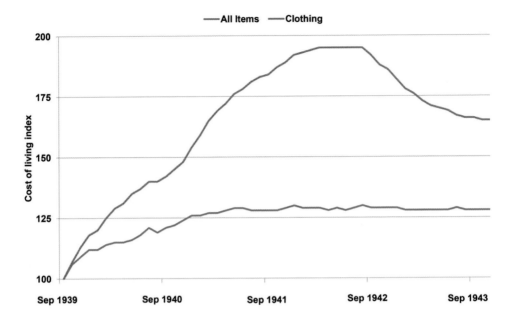

COMPARATIVE RISE IN THE COST OF LIVING INDEX SEPTEMBER 1939–DECEMBER 1943
Clothing was only one of the items which made up the cost of living index. The graph shows clearly how until the start of 1942 (and the arrival of Utility clothing in the shops) the cost of clothing was rising much faster than the norm, but from that point it flattened out, and by the end of the year was actually falling.

year of war. As time went on, however, shortages became more noticeable, exacerbated by the destruction in the Blitz of the great textile warehouse areas of London and Manchester.

As manufacturers were limited with regard to the amount they could produce, many turned to higher-end products, which made more profit. The Government acted to ease demand by raising prices using purchase tax, but this only aggravated the problems for the less affluent.

Many in government were determined that any sacrifices should be fair. Oliver Lyttelton, who had become President of the Board of Trade in October 1940, wanted to introduce clothes rationing, but Churchill was deeply set against it. Then, in 1941, while the Prime Minister was engrossed in the hunt for the German battleship Bismarck, Lyttelton slipped the idea through.

On Whit Sunday, 1 June 1941, Lyttleton announced that clothes rationing would begin next day. Thus, the impending rationing was kept secret. The **Sunday Express** claimed it was 'one of the most closely kept secrets in British history', although the

COUPONLESS LASS—
—NOT IN THE SWIM

" What can I do ? "
" Use moth-balls next time ! "

LEFT Under the system of rationing clothes had to last, and an enemy had to be overcome – the moth!

newspaper also reported, *'There was quite a minor boom in London shopping yesterday. At one shop specialising in women's clothes a Sunday Express reporter was told: "During the past few days there has been a marked increase in the number of customers".'*

Rationed items were given a coupon value, irrespective of price, related broadly to the square yardage of material involved; two coupons per square yard of cotton or rayon, and three for wool (later reduced to two). So, for example, a woollen dress required 11 coupons, whether it cost 30s or 50 guineas. While rationing did dampen demand, it did little to deal with the shortage of cheaper clothes.

Clothing rationing was very tight. The press suggested ways of coping; many providing annual clothes lists for men. It was generally agreed that women used more clothes than men and the **Sunday Express** found it impossible to make an annual allowance of 66 coupons stretch far enough. Its answer was to divide

RIGHT Utility nightdress, with the number 1106/2. The 'stroke two' indicates that it was sold as a two-piece set – probably with matching knickers. 1106 is an early (August 1942 onwards) four-figure number denoting that it is made of a rayon-type cloth (Numbers 1000-1206).

women's requirements into two lists – those items that were needed every year, including nightdress, underwear, shoes, stockings and (interestingly) gloves, and another list which rotated every three years, which included dresses, suits and coats.

In 1942 it was decided to cut the ration by about a quarter. The number of coupons was reduced to 60, but they had to last for 15 months instead of a year, equivalent to an annual total of 48. In 1943 coupon allowances fell to 47, in 1944 to 46, and again in 1945 to 41, due to the need for demob clothing. They rose in 1946 to 52, falling to 50 in 1947. The last coupons were issued in September 1948, with clothes rationing ending in March 1949.

The desired effect was achieved; demand slackened. However, rationing had other unintended effects. Some items were seen as unnecessary or 'coupon expensive'; women's pyjamas – a popular response to the unpredictability of night-time air raid warnings – required eight coupons as opposed to a nightdress at six. Siren suits at 11 coupons soon gave way to slacks, and for men, a waistcoat at five coupons was easily replaced by a jumper, knitted with recycled wool for nothing. A second consequence would not become obvious until mid-1943, as people realised that if you could only buy, for example, one suit a year it was better to buy an expensive suit which would last.

OPPOSITE PAGE AND ABOVE Heavy, double-breasted utility overcoat, numbered X227B. The X denotes 'Super Utility' – the most expensive grade of utility (January 1948 on), 227 is a heavy wool cloth, used for men's and youths' suits, jackets, trousers and overcoats.

The Utility Scheme

In spite of rationing, good-quality cheap clothing remained scarce and prices continued to rise. The Government considered several schemes, including buying civilian clothes to sell via the trade, employing a similar strategy with cloth, or forcing manufacturers to make specific items. In the end it decided to encourage them with raw material allocations to produce particular garments from particular cloths at prices to be clearly specified at each stage of production and distribution.

In June 1941 the Board of Trade set up the Directorate of Civilian Clothing *'to deal with questions arising on supply and distribution and to make whatever arrangements were necessary to ensure that adequate supplies of clothing, and in particular working-class clothing, were available for the population.'* In July Metford Watkins was appointed Director General of the Directorate. At the end of that month a secret Board memo stated: *'…the whole problem is exceedingly urgent and difficult. There will inevitably be a shortage of warm clothing for the working classes this winter unless the Director General:-*

1)   influences raw material allocation.

2)   regulates the present movement of labour away from the clothing trades.

3)   retards the tendency of manufacturers, wholesalers and retailers, on a diminished quantity turnover, to 'trade up' and leave high and dry the lower range of supply.'

No other appointments were made in the short term, the day-to-day work being carried out by civil servants, but three businessmen were asked to assist the Director General as 'directors' on a part-time, unpaid basis. These were Mr L Foyster, merchandise manager of Marks and Spencer (Deputy to Watkins), Clifford Williams (adviser on the woollen industry and men's clothing) and Tom Heron (adviser on other textiles and women's and children's clothing). The recently-appointed Director of Civilian Footwear at the Ministry of Supply, Mr H. G. Durston, was also transferred to the Board to rationalise the situation.

OPPOSITE PAGE Late utility shirt-dress. The alternative to plain material to avoid large pattern repeats was a busy, multi-coloured pattern such as this, where overlaps become almost invisible. An additional bonus is that the dress will go with a range of coats or accessories.

A Portland Utility shoe advertisement from December 1942.

Portland give Utility something extra

That 'something' is extra comfort, for Portland Utility shoes have the margin of extra width skilfully concealed, a feature that makes all the difference to women 'on the go' from morn 'till night.

P 6267
In Black or Brown Glace Kid. Shape 30.
Extra Wide Fitting. Built heel
1¼ in. high.

Portland STYLE · COMFORT SHOES

● Because of war-time restrictions you cannot be sure of getting any one particular model at your Portland Stockist's, but you can be sure of getting full-time comfort from whichever style you select.

Write ... ...pence in stamps for illustrated price list and name of your nearest stockist.
...S LTD. (DEPT. 71), PORTLAND SHOE WORKS, LEICESTER

ABOVE Whilst controlled, utility shoes were not standardised, as can be seen in the two very different styles shown in the advertisment and the photograph.

On 12 July, at his first press conference, Watkins said that he was planning to put back on sale clothes that were within the reach of working-class people. The type of clothing would be what was referred to as 'general utility', i.e. everyday wear. The first step would be a man's suit, of guaranteed quality material, at about 65s for tweed and 75s for worsted. These, he hoped, would be available in about three months. He also planned to extend the idea to children's clothes, women's underclothing, and eventually frocks. He stressed, however, that he did not want to introduce standardisation. *'We have to take care that people who cannot afford expensive clothes can get the things they want. We are making special arrangements to release cloth to go into these suits and we shall control the price all the way to the consumer under new legislation which I hope will come into force next week.*

'The cloth, which will be stamped by the manufacturers so that it can be recognised, will be guaranteed and will have a minimum standard of quality. There will be a wide range of design and colour. It will not be possible to fix a maximum price for the suits of that material made to measure.

'Its entire object is to provide all the financial and economic advantages of standardisation without the psychological disadvantages. So let us call it a "Watkins Suit" instead, in no sense will it be civilian uniform.'

An early Utility cloth advertisement from April 1942, giving some idea of the range of colours available.

Ten days later it was announced that 'National' boots and shoes costing less than fashion footwear would soon be introduced; the quality, price and style were to be approved by Durston. **The Times** reported 'a leading footwear manufacturer' as saying: *'The proposed 'national" lines will not oust fashion footwear from the market completely, but there may be a fairly large margin between the prices of the utility line and fashion goods.'* As this shows, at this early stage the terms 'Utility' and 'National' were interchangeable, leading to contemporary descriptions of the Utility symbol as 'the National Mark'.

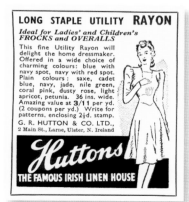

The Utility scheme began with the cloth. This advertisement for Utility rayon dates from January 1943.

'Celanese' still means Quality

Be careful!
A little thought, a little care
Will Save your Fuel and Underwear!
Warm water, and a gentle squeeze
Will quickly launder 'Celanese'
And then, because a cool iron's best,
You save heat, too, when it is pressed.

SAVE HEAT TO SAVE FUEL!

A Celanese advertisement from September 1943 – the use of the Utility label shows that it did not carry the stigma at this time that it did post-war.

The new clothing was going to take some time to filter through to the public, so from July, as a stopgap measure in what was dubbed the 'essential clothing scheme', the Board freed the cheaper types of cloths and clothing from quota control. According to the **Tailor and Cutter**, *'the Government, feeling that the supply of cheap clothing was not equal to the demand, made arrangements which encouraged firms to trade in such goods.'*

At the end of August, the **Tailor and Cutter** reported that *'standard cloth for women's clothes may be available by December says Board of Trade'*. It would be 75 per cent wool and 25 per cent cotton, *'and not too bad to look at'*. The magazine also dubbed the new female attire 'Watkins' Costumes'.

At the same time a simplified system of clothing control was announced. **The Times** explained: *'This simplification of the Government control of the cloth and clothing trades is part of the long-term plan of the Director General of Clothing to provide a range of clothing the public needs at the prices they can afford. Special quotas, which are considerably higher than the quotas under the old Order, are now to be assigned to manufacturers for the making of certain cloths, hose, and other knitted wear required to ensure an adequate supply of clothing of the general grades, particularly in the lower ranges of price.*

'This utility clothing is therefore to have first call on the available supplies of raw material. Manufacturers will be required to label with an appropriate identification mark all the cloth and clothing they supply under the special quotas. Makers-up will not be allowed to use the marked cloth except for the production of garments of utility grades. Prices of goods bearing the mark will be subject to special control.'

OPPOSITE PAGE Woman's utility housecoat or dressing gown, made of crepe. The label (right) bears the number 105 followed by 7 or 2. This denotes the material as a type of rayon. The embroidered flowers across the shoulders are very much of the post-war period.

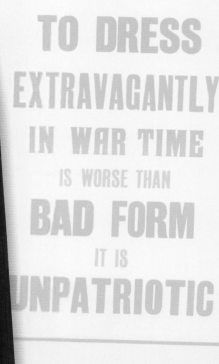

TO DRESS EXTRAVAGANTLY IN WAR TIME IS WORSE THAN BAD FORM IT IS UNPATRIOTIC

Men's trousers. The earliest utility and maker's labels were separate, but some manufacturers soon had special labels incorporating both their brand name and the utility mark. Note the absence of a number.

RIGHT Men's and boy's Utility underwear, 1943: (left) boy's wool and cotton vest (costing 5s 8d, two coupons), wool and cotton trunks (4s 10d, five coupons) and wool and cotton socks (2s 7d, one coupon); (right) man's interlock cotton vest (2s 3d, four coupons), interlock cotton short pants (2s 3d, four coupons) and wool socks (2s 7d, two coupons). Clearly, coupons were not related to price, but to factors such as amount and type of material, labour required, etc.

The Government had managed to ensure large supplies of cloth for their purpose, without forcing manufacturers to make it, by implementing a double system of supply quotas. This consisted of a small general quota and a much higher 'special' quota for 'Utility' cloth. The system ensured that Utility clothes would be relatively widely available as the cloth could only be used for such clothing.

On 2 September 1941 the Order came into effect. It introduced 40 simply described cloths (16 cotton, 19 wool, four woven rayon, and one locknit). The early, vague specifications meant that some of the cloth produced was of very poor quality, leading to complaints and a general tightening of specifications.

The Order also introduced the Utility mark. Along with the manufacturer's own label, it was to be printed on or attached to all cloth, clothing and shoes produced under the scheme, the number on the label referring to the cloth rather than the garment. Known colloquially at the Board as the cheeses, the mark was designed by Reginald Shipp. People always asked: what does it stand for? Certainly, at the introduction of the scheme, the Board insisted that it stood for nothing; the booklet 'The Utility Cloth and Clothings Scheme' describing how **'the Utility mark, which was designed to have no special meaning, but was merely distinctive.'** On 26 September the **Daily Mirror** described it as a *'national monogram'*. On 13 November the same paper informed its readers, *'How will you know Utility cloth or clothing? It will be marked or labelled very clearly in black and white or in a colour. The*

RIGHT Women's and girls' Utility underwear, 1943: (left to right) a woman's wool vest (costing 4s 2½d and three coupons) and wool panties (3s 11d and three coupons); girl's wool vest (4s ½d and two coupons) and rayon lock-knit panties (3s 4d and two coupons); small girl's wool vest (3s 6½d and one coupon) and wool knickers (1s 5½d and one coupon).

design of the label will in all cases be the same and include the figure 41 which refers to the current year.'

So what about the CC – did no-one ask the Board what it meant? Of course they did, but they were told that it was just a symbol. Some, however, were either misinformed, or else made up a different explanation. The accompanying advertisement from December 1941 has the Utility label standing for GC41 – with the GC designating Government Control! One month later the same advert appeared without the GC lettering. However, during the same month the **Derby Daily Telegraph** commented, *'If it were not for the little ticket marked "G.C. 41" you would never realise that the attractive dress with the American-styled skirt is a Utility frock.'* Other explanations say it stands for Civilian Clothing, Cloth Control, Controlled Commodity, etc. The same debate surrounds the origin of the name D-Day, and once again, the D in this instance actually has no meaning.

LEFT Very early Utility Goray skirt advert, December 1941. Of most interest is the picture of the Utility mark, and the (incorrect) description of it in the text.

OPPOSITE PAGE Woman's suit. It's cloth number, 209, is one of the earliest, referring to 'medium weight wool', coming in a range of colours, plain, pinstripe, herringbone, etc.

Women's Utility pyjamas, 1943. Night bombing raids, and the consequent need
to get to the shelters quickly, saw women's pyjamas rise in popularity.

A Board Order of 12 September fixed maximum wholesale prices of men's and boys' Utility suits, overcoats, jackets, trousers and raincoats, woollen, cotton, and rayon cloths and knitted underwear, much of which would not be on sale for some time. Metford Watkins observed, *'All I have done is to bring in a system of price control and to see that cheaper cloth was made, and that the cheaper cloth was not made into expensive suits.'* General Utility suits would actually cost about 5s less than the 65s retail price originally quoted. Ready-made suits of the best cloth would cost approximately 96s 6d, and made-to-measure 109s.

Ten days later the **Hull Daily Mail** reported that *'The cloths and garments will in no way be "standard articles" as the more efficient manufacturers and makers will have enough scope to enable them to give individuality to the cloths and garments which they make.'* Watkins told the press: *'One thing I want to emphasise is that I do not want standard clothes. The suits for men and women, which will be on sale towards the end of next month, are not "Watkins suits", "Standard suits", "Utility suits" or "Civilian uniform".'*

In October, the **Gloucester Journal** reported on new women's underwear: *'No frills and little, if any, lace, will be found on the controlled-price underwear. These will be known as "utility" garments. I learn that prices will range from 4s 6d to 7s 5d for vests, 8s 8d to 14s 10d for nightdresses, and 11s 4d to 15s 9d for pyjamas. Fabrics being used for this special underwear are rayon locknit, plain,*

THE HOUSE OF ARROWSMITH.

Odd Coppers

You may have wondered at the unusual prices at which 'Utility' merchandise is marked. Everything bearing the official 'Utility' label may only be sold at the price specified by the Board of Trade. Prices are fixed through all stages of production, and are calculated on a controlled percentage basis at all stages, and, if it comes out at an odd copper, it just has to remain at that price, which is the maximum permitted.

Arrowsmiths
of ASHINGTON
ASHINGTONS' SHOPPING CENTRE   PHONE 83

An interesting description of the early Utility pricing arrangements, which would later be simplified.

dyed or printed with semi-bright or bright finish, woven rayon, crepe de chine, crepe satin, spun rayon and wynceyette.'

By now the word Utility was being used for the scheme as a whole, the individual items of clothing, and the CC41 mark. Each Utility garment was made in three grades. They roughly corresponded to basic, medium and high-end, depending on the weight, or quality, of material used, so each had a range of maximum prices depending on the grade.

Two days later, the **Daily Mirror** explained the Utility scheme to its readers in these terms: 'From now on all cloth and clothing is to be divided into two groups – Utility and General.

'What garments are covered by the scheme? All essential clothes, although there are some modifications in the case of corsets for example. There is a feeling that very cheap corsets would not be an economy, but a plan will be arranged for them. Lingerie of every description, suits, dresses, overcoats, skirts and blouses, are some of the garments included. Cloths by the yard include tweeds of several weights, woollen and worsted mixtures, grey union flannel, winceyette, drill gingham, rayons, lock-knit fabric.

'Do not think fashion will disappear with the coming of Utility clothes. There will be strong competition amongst designers and manufacturers to offer good style and fit – more than if the materials and prices were decontrolled.

'All clothing not included in the Utility group comes under the 'general' heading, and these can be sold at higher prices. Most shops will have materials and garments in this group, although there will not be so many of them as there are now.'

It is interesting to note the two categories of clothing described in the article: Utility and General. The second term saw little use; soon the two chosen descriptions were almost universally Utility and non-Utility.

Less than a week later it was announced that the Board had fixed maximum prices for women's and girls' coats, skirts, costumes, and slacks under the Utility scheme. Maximum retail prices (including purchase tax) ranged from 17s 3d to 26s 3d for skirts, 21s to 31s 1d for slacks, 63s to 95s 2d for coats, and from 65s 2d to 86s 2d for costumes.

In November 1941, in an address to Parliament, Sir Andrew Duncan, President of the Board of Trade, spelt out the maximum gross percentage profits which wholesalers and

Just four weeks after the introduction of the Utility scheme, Derry and Toms were selling utility coats. Actually the term 'utility' here relates to the early meaning of 'general use' and certainly not to Utility scheme garments, which did not arrive until 1942. In April 1942 it became illegal to use the word in trade descriptions or advertisements relating to cloth or apparel which were not part of the official scheme.

retailers were permitted under the scheme. Manufacturers' profits could not exceed 4 per cent on top of production and sales costs. *'For a wholesaler the margin allowed on utility clothing must not exceed 20 per cent of the price at which he buys from the manufacturer. For a retailer it must not exceed 33 per cent of the price, including Purchase Tax, at which he buys from the wholesaler or manufacturer. In either case the price thus calculated must not exceed the selling price laid down for the goods in question by the relevant Order.'* This was known as the cost-plus method.

During November Sir Metford Watkins resigned as Director-General of Civilian Clothing, and was replaced by Sir Thomas Barlow. The **Tailor and Cutter** announced that *'the Board of Trade plan for providing clothing at prices which most people can afford to pay is now taking shape'*.

Concentration and Designation

War demanded a restructuring of industry. Raw materials had to be channelled away from 'luxury' products. This was done through a combination of LIMOSOs, the levying of purchase tax, and rationing, leaving many factories working below capacity. Concentration of industry was an idea developed in 1940 to release labour and factory-space for essential production by running a few factories at full capacity while the remainder closed.

Sir Cecil Weir, Controller General of Factory and Storage Premises, described the process: *'They must get together in two's or three's or four's and submit individual schemes whereby production would be concentrated in one factory of the group – the*

OPPOSITE PAGE AND ABOVE Utility pinafore. A small but busy pattern such as this, could be joined together without matching up, thereby saving material.

ABOVE A spinning 'mule' in front of ranks of its brethren in 1942. Such spinning machines had driven the Industrial Revolution that unfolded in Britain's 'dark satanic mills' during the 19th century.

OPPOSITE PAGE Typical Utility cloth pattern for women's dresses, etc. Flowers and foliage were very popular, and the blend of colours meant that it could be matched with a range of accessories, coats, etc.

"nucleus unit" – with such transfers to the nucleus unit of older and experienced labour and machines from the closing factories as might be necessary.' Nucleus firms had to employ at least 50 workers full-time. Voluntary aggregation into nucleus firms was encouraged generally, but in industries such as textiles and footwear it was compulsory. Firms which closed down would be given a cut of the profits and every opportunity to regain trade after the war, when their revival would be helped by the enormous demand for goods that would then occur.

Concentration was accomplished by dint of Government orders; in October 1941 the Government announced that women would be called up into the forces or to work in 'essential' industry. The **Daily Mail** reported that *'The big call-up announced on Monday of all young women aged 20–25 in the light clothing industry means that very soon now luxury clothes and exclusively dressed women will disappear "for the duration". By next summer, or autumn at the latest, Britain's stocks of women's clothes will be exhausted.'* The light clothing industry produced women's, children's and infants' garments, and the heavy industry made men's suits, overcoats and shirts, and women's overcoats.

Once again, the Board acted to protect the Utility scheme. In mid-November **The Times** reported that *'Firms which comply with special conditions will be "designated" by the Board of Trade. In the "light" section of the trade "designation" will be given to firms engaged 75% or more on the production of clothing of general utility. They will have all their female labour, including the women in the 20 to 25 age group, protected. Both in the "light" and "heavy" sections of the trade there will also be designation for firms engaged 75% or more on utility clothing and government and export orders combined, and they will have protection for their*

There are no frills or fancies about Lybro Utility Overalls, these days. But there's working comfort . . . and first-rate service. That's why they're so popular—and sometimes so scarce!

LYBRO
UTILITY
OVERALLS

ABOVE Women's overalls, June 1943. There were increasing numbers of women required for factory work.

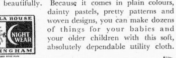

The finest Utility cloth you can buy—

Here's a cloth that is completely reliable — it carries the famous "Day & Night Wear" guarantee of quality. 'Dayella' is shrink-resisting and hard-wearing, and washes beautifully. Because it comes in plain colours, dainty pastels, pretty patterns and woven designs, you can make dozens of things for your babies and your older children with this soft, absolutely dependable utility cloth.

LEFT An advertisement from November 1942 clearly showing the Utility mark with the specification number 210. This was a cloth for *'women's and maid's* [young women's] *costumes'.*

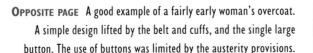

OPPOSITE PAGE A good example of a fairly early woman's overcoat. A simple design lifted by the belt and cuffs, and the single large button. The use of buttons was limited by the austerity provisions.

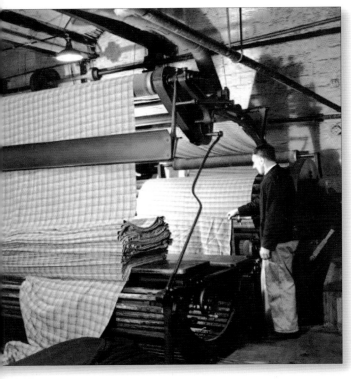

LEFT A mill worker supervising a facing machine in April 1942. This machine brushed a light pile onto the material, which in this case was a lady's Utility checked material made from 75-year-old reclaimed wool.

female labour, excepting only the women in the 20 to 25 age group.'

Further, their premises could not be command-eered for more important war work, as could happen to non-designated firms. Designated Utility producers would receive most of the cloth allocated for civilian clothing, and thus virtually guaranteed sales. Naturally this made designation extremely desirable. **The Times** observed: *'How many firms will obtain designation is a little uncertain, but the number will probably lie between 600 and 800, employing approximately 80,000 people.'*

In January 1942 firms were invited to apply for designation. The Board selected those which, in their opinion, employed the most efficient production methods, which generally meant an assembly line as opposed to the more traditional 'making-through' method, where one worker made the entire garment. By March there were 1,200 designated producers out of a total of 30,000 manufacturers. The July figures show designation was increasing – there were now 2,000 – and also the success of concentration with only 25,000 manufacturers remaining.

Concentration of the clothing industry first took place in London and Leeds, but in November 1942 the scheme was extended throughout the country. Although concentration and designation were wartime expedients, the resulting promotion of mass-production ensured that the post-war British clothing industry was far better prepared to compete in export markets.

OPPOSITE PAGE Utility tweeds and homespuns advertisement, September 1943.

LADIES *Shoes*

UT115   W3 os/H

LONDON/TAN   Z398

6½

Footwear

At the beginning of December 1941 the Board announced that
'"National-mark" footwear will be available in the new year, and some 50 to 60% of the 8,500,000 pairs manufactured under concentration of the industry will be of utility lines. These, it is understood, will be in three ranges – low, medium and better grades.' In March 1942 it was announced that they should be available in June.

At the end of May, the Board announced that from June at least 50 per cent of each boot and shoe manufacturer's production had to be of Utility footwear, but it added that they would not be immediately available to the public. A leading manufacturer commented: *'It will be useless for the public to expect to buy purchase tax-free Utility shoes on June 1. We have not yet received the specifications. There will only be a trickle of Utility footwear in June, but production should mount rapidly after that.'*

On 9 July the **Aberdeen Journal** announced that *'Utility footwear is expected to be on sale in a fortnight. One hundred and fifteen specifications have been approved. They include industrial clogs, miners' boots and steel-fitted toe-caps, agricultural boots, moulders' boots and some special footwear. All Utility footwear must have a leather upper, and there will be no cardboard insole.*

'Prices will be graded up to a maximum of £2. Materials used will be all normal leathers, including calf, glace kid and suede. The Utility mark "CC41" will be stamped on the footwear, probably on the sole.'

RIGHT A shoe advertisement from October 1942, when the first utility shoes were arriving in the shops.

OPPOSITE PAGE A pair of women's utility shoes with their original box. This shows three numbers: UT115, W3, and Z398, representing the makers' number, the price range, and the utility specification.

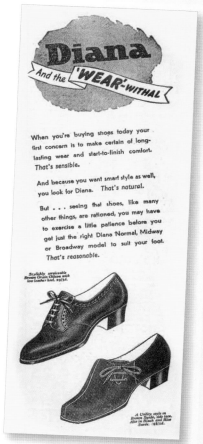

Diana
And the **'WEAR'**-WITHAL

When you're buying shoes today your first concern is to make certain of long-lasting wear and start-to-finish comfort. That's sensible.

And because you want smart style as well, you look for Diana. That's natural.

But . . . seeing that shoes, like many other things, are rationed, you may have to exercise a little patience before you get just the right Diana Normal, Midway or Broadway model to suit your foot. That's reasonable.

ABOVE AND LEFT Some utility footwear had a version of the utility stamp pressed into the sole, such as these, in mock alligator skin. The heels of this pair are verging on the maximum height allowed – 2 ⅛ inches.

In Parliament on 23 July, the Minister of Economic Warfare Hugh Dalton announced that *'Utility footwear is coming along very well and is much praised by those who have seen it and worn it, but it is not yet in the shops in substantial quantities, although I hope that it will be in a few months' time.'* In August crepe rubber soles, metal buckles and rubber adhesive in shoe manufacture were prohibited, as was the use of cut-outs such as open-toes. Heels could be no taller than 2 1/8 inches and made of wood without any leather covering.

At the beginning of October advertisements trumpeted that *'Utility shoes just arrived!'* In December, the **Western Gazette** reported: *'In spite of their simplicity they have distinctive characteristics – some are laced at the side, some have galosh toes, or high tongues, and many have attractively placed stitching, or raised seams. There are court slip-on shoes, too, with medium or slightly higher heels, some with leather buckles, others with light brogue-stitching.'*

Children's shoes were a particular problem. In the House of Commons, Labour MP Manny Shinwell said that children's Utility shoes were generally very expensive, quite unsuitable in wintertime, and were made of *'rubbishy material'*. In September

RIGHT This early advertisement dates from October 1942.

BELOW Late utility sandals. The platform sole became popular towards the latter end of the war and after. The open-toe was only allowed after 1947.

Clarks
SHOES

Sold by selected retailers all over the country. If you cannot find the "Utility" shoe illustrated (in marbled kid), please choose another Clarks style from your retailer's stock.

ON THE WAY . . . Clarks, who have been making beautiful shoes since 1825 have in production a range of Utility Footwear. All manufacturers have to conform to a standard of quality in the materials used for Utility Footwear, but when you buy Clarks Utility shoes you are assured of more than this. You are assured also of that skill in designing and workmanship which has been their pride for over a century. MADE BY C. & J. CLARK LTD., (WHOLESALE ONLY), STREET, SOMERSET, *and by Clarks (Ireland) Ltd., Dundalk*

Unusual late forties'
house shoes or slippers,
with impressed utility
mark on the leather sole.

1943 the **Aberdeen Journal** reported that they were causing absenteeism in the schools. *'One Wick headmaster said a pupil had worn out a pair of Utility boots in a fortnight.'* Three weeks later Dalton addressed the matter in Parliament: *'I have decided that, as from 1st November, all outdoor footwear, non-Utility as well as Utility, shall bear the maker's identification mark. I have also decided to increase to 75 per cent the proportion of children's shoes which must be made according to Utility specification.'*

In the first week of June 1946 the Board announced that, as from July, manufacturers could produce the kind and quantities of shoes they wanted, subject to two conditions – that half of their production of adult footwear and three-quarters of their production of children's footwear should be Utility, and that they should not make fewer children's shoes than they did in the first quarter of the year.

In mid-May 1947 the 'cover the foot' requirement was removed, as was the limitation on the number of pieces of upper material. Further, stiffeners and puffs could be omitted if the style required.

In mid-August 1948 the **Western Morning News** reported that *'…considerable changes in the Utility footwear scheme were announced. They will come into effect on September 27. The old specifications are being replaced by 3 new grades numbered 1, 2 and 3 – for each type of shoe, with corresponding controlled prices. Slippers and house shoes and shoes with fabric uppers are being brought into the Utility range, as well as shoes incorporating fur or sheepskin. A minimum amount of material and workmanship is laid down for such types in grades 1 and 2.'*

Devonshire
LADIES' SHOES

WITH points for this and coupons for that, the question of what is wise expenditure is best answered by the "DEVONSHIRE" range of utility shoes. Here is value if ever there was ! They're stylish and comfortable and give that lasting wear that everyone wants. Besides, they're in such variety that wartime limitations seem to vanish.

MOLLY CHOSE THEM FOR *ECONOMY*

MAISIE CHOSE THEM FOR *STYLE*

MAUD CHOSE THEM FOR *COMFORT*

ANOTHER SMART UTILITY DESIGN

Brown Grain Gibson. Contrasting Brown Suede Saddle.

The price is fixed in accordance with the directions of The Board of Trade as issued in connection with National Utility Footwear.

THE MANSFIELD SHOE CO., LTD., MANSFIELD, NOTTS.

LEFT Utility shoe advertisement from November 1942, stressing Economy, Style, and Comfort. Comfort was important; strict petrol rationing meant that 'shank's pony' was the only means of getting around.

BELOW Austerity provisions, and a general lack of transport, meant that by the late forties, women's shoe styles had evolved into a low wedge shape — but the fifties, and 'Florentine' stilettos, were on the way.

Utility in Operation
November 1941 to June 1942

By the end of November 1941, samples of women's Utility clothing were on show. The **Western Times** reported: *'Charming in design and colouring the Government's "Utility" cloths that are now being distributed to retailers will be a real boon to all who desire the best value for the expenditure of their money – and what is equally important, their coupons. Some of the garments are marked "C.C." – these are the least expensive, but their style is as smart as the higher priced article. Skirts of black woollen material, for instance, pleated, range from 9s to 14s 11d, and well-cut slacks, which women are finding admirable for warmth, while working in the home or garden, can be had for 12s 6d. Even in the more expensive category of Utility clothes, it is possible to buy a delightfully warm winter coat, fashioned with un-pressed pleats at the back to the waist, a tie belt and large pockets for less than £5.'*

The **Dundee Evening Telegraph** remarked that *'Colours are beautiful. The ruling powers have provided 45 shades and if a woman can't find anything to her satisfaction from these she should join one of the services and give up the thought of fashions for the duration.'*

ABOVE A display of Utility clothes, all designed by Norman Hartnell, 1942. Featured on the display stand are two dresses, the one on the right costing 60s. Behind them is a rail of 'Berkertex Utility frocks', and to the right, a rail of skirts.

OPPOSITE PAGE A typical light, summer-style utility frock. The detail is created by the white collar and looped edging.
LEFT As with so many printed Utility labels, this one has faded, so it is impossible to read the specification number.

The public were unimpressed with the name 'Utility'. In December, the **Press and Journal** commented, '*Ask yourself and any friend what the words "utility garments" convey – the answer is always much the same "Some kind of cross between a union suit and dungarees, which we shall probably all soon be wearing." Nothing could be further from the truth.*' In April 1942 the **Tailor and Cutter** added, '*One wonders who chose the word "Utility" for the suits sponsored by the Board of Trade. It was an unlucky word and failed to appeal from the first. There is no glamour about Utility in clothes and, whatever the male may think certainly the word would not appeal to women.*' That month an Order decreed that '*The word "Utility", or any word resembling it, may not be employed in trade descriptions or advertisements relating to cloth or apparel, which is not part of the Utility scheme.*'

Towards the end of February 1942, Hugh Dalton was appointed President of the Board of Trade. That month the **Yorkshire Post** and **Leeds Mercury** reported on '*the latest development of the black market trade, which is directed towards Utility clothing. The Board of Trade have found evidence that unscrupulous retailers have been removing the official label from Utility suits and selling the articles at considerably more than the controlled prices.*'

For the time being the resources of Braemar are almost entirely devoted to Utility Knitwear only. Classic round-necked, short and long-sleeved jumpers and cardigans are being made to utility specifications in a range of six lovely colours. The name 'Braemar' on each garment is an assurance that it has been made by the finest and most individual wool craftsmen in the world.

INNES, HENDERSON & CO. LTD.
HAWICK · SCOTLAND

From the new Spring range of Alexon Coats and Suits comes this superbly tailored Utility Model, available at leading Fashion Houses.

WHOLESALE: ALEXON & CO. LTD.
120/2 ALDERSGATE STREET · LONDON · E.C.1

A Utility suit from March 1944.

LEFT Utility knitwear, like hosiery and corsetry, had to conform to specifications for the garment, and not just for the cloth. This dates from December 1944.

OPPOSITE PAGE Detail of the dress on page 52. The deep orange on the buttons is caused by the rusting of their cheap inner piece.

In the budget of 17 April the Chancellor Sir Kingsley Wood made an announcement which gave Utility clothing a huge boost. All Utility cloth and clothing would be exempt from purchase tax from September, and the same exemption would apply to boots and shoes later on. On the other hand tax on 'luxury' articles was doubled to 66 2/3 per cent with immediate effect.

Dalton welcomed the announcement: *'We will see that the consumer gets the benefit of it. A man's wool vest costs with the tax 15s, 1s 8d will come off, making it 13s 4d. The policy of the Government is to make luxury prices rise, and I shall not worry much about them.'* By now about two-thirds of all cloth produced was going into Utility clothing; Dalton's aim was to raise the proportion to 100 per cent.

On 30 April it was announced that *'Women's and maids'* [teenagers'] *dresses and blouses are brought into the "Utility" clothes scheme by the Civilian Clothing (Restrictions) No. 6 Order which comes into force on June 20'*. New restrictions were introduced that applied to the manufacture of both Utility and non-Utility garments made by professional dressmakers as well as commercial manufacturers. Dresses could not have tiered skirts, external epaulettes, capes, turn-back cuffs, imitation pockets, buttons on pockets, non-functional buttons or slide fasteners. They could not have more than two pockets, five buttons and buttonholes for any openings except on coat-frock or button-through dresses, where buttons might be placed along the opening at intervals of not less than 4 inches, with not more than one button and buttonhole on each sleeve.

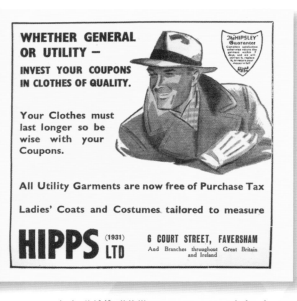

WHETHER GENERAL OR UTILITY –

INVEST YOUR COUPONS IN CLOTHES OF QUALITY.

Your Clothes must last longer so be wise with your Coupons.

All Utility Garments are now free of Purchase Tax

Ladies' Coats and Costumes. tailored to measure

HIPPS (1931) LTD   6 COURT STREET, FAVERSHAM
And Branches throughout Great Britain and Ireland

In April 1942 all Utility garments were made free from purchase tax, a measure which gave sales a huge boost.

OPPOSITE PAGE Typical utility summer frock. With its short, puff sleeves, and lack of pleats, the main body of the dress is very plain, but it is lifted by the white collar and covered buttons, the heart shaped pocket, and upper seams picked out by the white piping. Simple, yet effective.

Above From the cradle to the grave — a very small baby's utility dress. Like most such dresses it is very long; no attempt has been made to skimp on material, in this case a type of rayon. Cheap and well-made, utility was extremely popular for children's clothes.

Sleeves had to have a maximum circumference of 14 inches at the wrist, collars a maximum width of 5 inches, and waist-belts and hems, 2 inches. No more than six seams were allowed in a woollen skirt and seven in a non-woollen one. Rules for pleats dictated no more than two inverted or box-pleats, or four knife-pleats in sizes up to 44-inch hips or four inverted or box-pleats or six knife-pleats in sizes above 44

ABOVE An advertisement for men's Utility shirts and pyjamas, December 1944.
RIGHT A Utility cardigan jacket from September 1943.

inches. No dress could have more than 160 inches in total of pin-tucking, hem-stitching, or bar-machine stitching, no ornamental stitching apart from collar and bodice front pleats, and no embroidery of any kind.

Similar rules applied to jumper-suits, which could have no more than two pockets, eight buttons, no collar or reveres, and a maximum cardigan length of 28 inches. Blouses were to have no more than one pocket, seven buttons and buttonholes on full-length sleeves, or five buttons and buttonholes on blouses without full-length sleeves.

Makers of women's and girls' underwear and nightwear could no longer use embroidery, appliqué work and similar decorations, or lace, including lace tops and motifs.

Men's shirts were to be 2 inches shorter and without double cuffs, while leather and metal buttons and overcoat belts were banned. Hugh Dalton estimated that the shortening of shirts and the elimination of double cuffs would save 4,000,000 square yards of material and the labour of 1,000 workers a year.

Lastly, not more than 50 sets of basic-style patterns could be used by any one manufacturer in a year. **Tit-Bits** magazine explained: *'One Hartnell design can be executed in ten different materials and twelve different colours. That gives 120 variations.*

A manufacturer, limited by Board of Trade rule to fifty models a year, can still, with his ten materials and twelve colours, provide 6,000 variations.'

Problems were beginning to appear – increased quotas had encouraged the manufacture of Utility cloth and clothing, but without any control being exerted over the sizes and types of items offered, so that there was often a concentration on the more popular sizes and styles. Further, in the Board's eagerness to encourage Utility production, firms had been given too much leeway with regard to quality.

In the early summer of 1942 control by quota was dropped and a new Apparel and Textiles Order was passed. This required manufacturers to comply with any

ABOVE Although not part of the original utility clothing scheme, first children's, and then babies' clothes were soon added. The 4-figure specification number, 1631B, shows this to be a later piece of utility.

1631B 12 TNH

ABOVE At first, hats were not included in the utility scheme, but, boys' caps, and girls' hat-and-overcoat combinations began to be included, and later woollen berets, and, from late 1944, men's flat caps could be made from utility material, thus carrying the utility mark.

directions regulating or prohibiting manufacture or supply. Now the Board could match demand and supply for particular types of clothing, estimating demand through consumer surveys and stocks and sales. In this way, production could be organised to meet anticipated demand.

TO DRESS
EXTRAVAGANT
IN WAR TIM
IS WORSE THAN
BAD FOR
IT IS
UNPATRIO

Wot – No Turn-ups?

In March 1942, the Making of Civilian Clothing (Restrictions) Order was passed, and it came into operation in May. Under its provisions, men's suits had to be single-breasted with no slits or buttons on the cuffs, flaps over the pockets, elastic in the trouser-waistband, zip fasteners or turn-ups. A limit was also put on the number of pockets and buttons.

At the beginning of March **The Times** commented, '*…the notion of "Utility clothing" may be accorded a sober but cordial welcome…the utility of clothing has long been too generally subordinated to its power of adornment….Now that the purpose of clothing is officially proclaimed to be utility there can be no harm in sparing a moderate amount of consideration to its other functions, including both adornment and comfort.*

'The new proposals give men a good opportunity of keeping up the old pretence that they do not care what they wear. Buttons on the cuffs of coat sleeves may go and welcome….There may be some slight danger of an increase in the use or the coat sleeve where the best manners prescribe a handkerchief; but the promised economy is worth the risk. When roads in town and country were as muddy as ploughed fields, it was necessary to turn up the bottoms of the trouser legs, which would take the mud on the inside and thus leave

OPPOSITE PAGE AND ABOVE Men's formal dinner suit. It was not the fashion to have turn-ups on such a suit, so they were not part of the turn-up controversy. The label (above) has the specification number: X (super-Utility) 209F (a variation on 209) /2 meaning it was part of a two-piece set, or in this case, suit.

LEFT Men trying on clothes from the Utility scheme range – trouser turn-ups had disappeared under the new spirit of austerity.

RIGHT Men's utility overcoat; the flap pockets and matching belt show it to be either very early, or post war, as otherwise they were banned.

the outside clean, to be turned down when the moment came. The turn-up survived the muddy roads into the age of asphalt, and, becoming a fiction, was not even an honest turn-up, but a mere tailored pretence. Let it go, by all means.'

Others took the whole thing less philosophically. On 6 April 1944 David Robertson, MP for Streatham, proclaimed: *'This interference with the liberty of the subject was not debated in this House, and was not decided upon by any Act. It was brought about by delegated legislation. The Statutory Rule and Order is signed by Mr Overton and it is on one half-sheet of paper, and yet it materially affected the habits and customs and the dress of every male, from youths to aged persons.'*

In March 1943 the **Dundee Courier** added its voice to a rumbling revolt over the banning of turn-ups – *'Even the tailors are not convinced of its justification. They have started a national campaign to convince the Government Department that the Utility trousers are highly unpopular. The lack of turn-ups sticks in the throat of men otherwise ready to swallow patriotically the privations of total war. [The law] authorises departmental inspectors actually to pry into private wardrobes in quest of illegal turn-ups or double-breasted suits. This sartorial snooping shows the intolerable growth of burocratic [sic] tyranny exercised purely for its own sake.'*

"Look, darling—I've cut off all the lapels and pocket patches and trouser turn-ups for you, so you'll be all right for style!"

The furore over men's suits, and especially their turn-ups, was a rich source of humour for cartoonists; this example comes from July 1942.

Tailors were consistently vocal in their opposition to the austerity provisions. Almost exactly two years earlier, Dalton had addressed the issue at a press conference. *'There are no turn-ups in either the Army, Navy or Air Force, and I should have thought a style that was good enough for the Fighting Forces should have been good enough for civilians in war-time. Nor do the Police and other wearers of uniform have turn-ups.*

BELOW Typical utility working shirt with attached collar, no breast pocket, and only opening at the neck, instead of the usual all-the-way-down, all to save on material, but more importantly, labour.

ABOVE Boy's utility shorts. The X specification number means that they are top-of-the-range, super-Utility. Note the buttons for braces. Sadly utility braces, containing no elastic, were one of the abject failures of the scheme.

'There can be no equality of sacrifice in this war. Some must lose lives and limbs; others only the turn-ups on their trousers.'

In the event the Army stepped in. Sir Cecil Weir, Director General of Equipment and Stores at the Ministry of Supply, wrote, 'While the war was still at its height we were planning for peace. What clothing should be given to the demobilized man? We would be no parties to sending demobilized men back home from their units in a suit that didn't fit, a sort of hand-me-down garment, supplemented only by Service shirts and boots.

'Our proposal was a simple one. It was to give to every demobilized officer and man a complete civilian outfit —a suit, an overcoat, or raincoat, a shirt, two collars and a tie, two pairs of socks, a hat and a pair of shoes.

'Should we attempt to include the Women's Services in our programme? Unanimous opinion: "No" – we could never satisfy the variety of women's tastes and in their case, with smaller numbers and a totally different problem, a money allowance would be the proper solution.'

The idea was that service heroes deserved to return home better dressed than they had departed; this did not mean a suit without turn-ups! Parliament approved the idea – who would dare speak against it? A few brave souls did – in the Commons, David Robertson, MP for Streatham, said 'I do not think there is anything too good we can give these men, but I think they will want a job and a home a little bit more than they will want a suit. I think that a fellow who has lived in a battle-dress for some years will not worry very much whether his trousers are turned up or turned down, or how many pockets there are in his waistcoat.'

Above A two-piece suit saved coupons, but the waistcoat hid the braces buttons, so many had their buttons inside, like this.

The Board decided that if both austerity and demob suits were produced, this situation would inevitably create a black market, with demobbed men being offered large sums for their non-austerity suits. Dalton felt that he must keep civilian clothing styles in line with those of ex-servicemen and it was decided to revoke the austerity order relating to men's and boys' clothes. It was later announced that boys' and youths' suits would not be included in the lifting of the regulations, and would continue to be made in the austerity style. Men's suits already manufactured would require fewer coupons, and the Ministry of Supply would purchase any unsold austerity suits for use in post-war reconstruction in occupied countries.

Demob suits were made under Government contract; manufacturers therefore received extra quotas of raw materials and cloth in the same way as Utility makers had done. However, they were not Utility clothes. Like them they bore identifying labels, which stated 'Demob'd Servicemen' and contained information on the type of garment, size, date of manufacture, and the armed services' arrow.

Opposite page A late, two-piece, man's flannel suit, in a casual, or 'sports' style. It retains some early restrictions; single-breasted, three-button front, but the three sleeve buttons and pocket flaps mark it as later.

The Couturier Scheme

Women's reaction to Utility clothes was in sharp contrast to men's. In June 1943 the Gloucester Journal commented: *'A kind of stocking controversy has been going on for some time between women and the Board of Trade. Most women have been complaining about the bad wear of Utility stockings. Other complaints made about Utility goods concern corsets, underwear and shoes. Some shoes, it is said, need soling too soon and some corsets take on the shape of the body instead of giving the body shape.*

'In all this, of course, we have to remember, "there is a war on." If, in some respects, clothing standards are not as high as they were in the beginning of the war, this, in a general way, is due to the unavailability of materials. Most women realise the position and feel, in all the circumstances, they are being very well served in the manner of dress.'

The complaints were very practical, about durability, and fitness for purpose; there was no demur at having to give up, for example, long dresses or pleats. Perhaps women were more open to changes of fashion, whereas men generally wore the same styles all their lives – under these circumstances change did not go down well.

Large-scale Utility production had been accomplished by designation, and low prices achieved through price control and exemption from purchase tax. The final

ABOVE A top-coat from the Incorporated Society of London Fashion Designers show. Each chosen designer was asked to produce a top-coat, suit, afternoon dress and cotton overall-dress, all from Utility fabric.

OPPOSITE PAGE The label reads; 'American Style Clothing'. Pre-war, it would have indicated French clothing, or 'modes', but with the fall of France, and British austerity, the US was seen as the world's fashion centre. Yet this is still a Utilty frock.

ABOVE A Ministry of Information photograph of models wearing items of clothing designed by members of the Incorporated Society of London Fashion Designers for the 'Couturier Scheme'.

hurdle was to change the public perception that Utility clothes were boring, boxy, shoddy and 'standardised'.

When the Board had set up the Directorate of Civilian Clothing in June 1941, it had asked Tom Heron to advise on women's and children's clothing. He was a perfect candidate for the job. As Managing Director of Cresta Silks, he was not only a firm believer in the desirability of high-quality clothing, but as a practitioner he was also commissioning top designers (including Paul Nash for textile design and Wells Coates for his shops). Furthermore, he was a committed socialist, thus combining in one person the three founding principles of the Utility scheme.

In May 1942, with a view to improving the image of women's Utility clothing, Heron invited members of the Incorporated Society of London Fashion Designers each to design a top-coat, suit, afternoon dress and a cotton overall-dress, all made from Utility fabric and conforming to the austerity regulations. The idea became

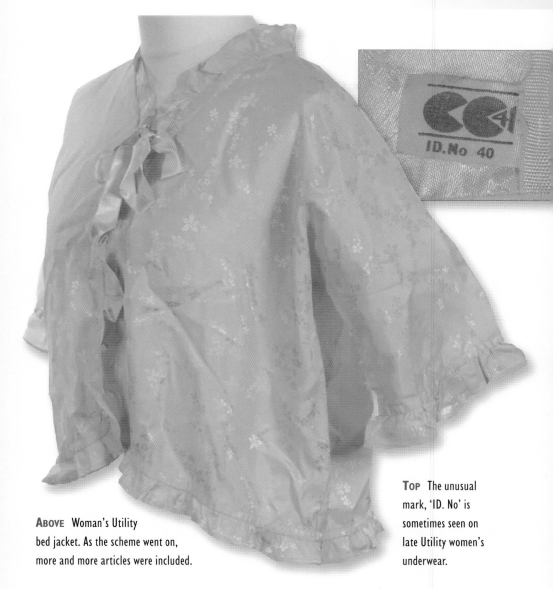

ABOVE Woman's Utility
bed jacket. As the scheme went on,
more and more articles were included.

TOP The unusual
mark, 'ID. No' is
sometimes seen on
late Utility women's
underwear.

known as 'the couturier scheme'. The designers involved were Hardy Amies, Creed, Bianca Mosca, Digby Morton, Peter Russell, Victor Stiebel, and Worth.

The resulting outfits were launched at a fashion show in September, alongside copies adapted for the trade. All the mannequins used were engaged on war work. Opening the show Sir Thomas Barlow, Director General of Civilian Clothing, said, *'This must be a minor historical event, for these models must be the first civilian clothing ever commissioned by the Government.'* Following the show, templates for use by the trade were produced, and (unusually) also for the home dressmaker.

The outfits received high-profile publicity. Amazingly, the main criticism was that the costumes were '*Too Mayfair and not sufficiently practical for the war-worker.*' The **Daily Mail** reported that '*The women of Britain cannot agree on the Board of Trade's new Utility styles. Those in London and the smart provincial centres are pleased, but the housewives and the girls in offices and factories fight shy of them. Even the women's wear trade is not agreed on the criticism. A manufacturer told me yesterday: "I consider most of the clothes practical and well designed. The criticism 'too Mayfair' justifies the Board of Trade's initiative. The Board is anxious that 'Utility' should not come to mean 'dowdy'. My experience is that women do not tire of well-designed and well-proportioned clothes."*'

ABOVE LEFT A particular feature of this suit is the cross-wise use of the checks on the skirt and 'pockets'.

ABOVE RIGHT Another dress from the Incorporated Society of London Fashion Designers.

ABOVE Gloves became controlled in late 1942. They were still regarded as essential for the well-dressed woman.

SPECIAL DELIVERY BY *Berkertex*

FLASH!

Sleekly cut—gaily practical —Norman Hartnell has specially created this charming Berkertex model in wool angora, with adaptable collar, not only for stock size fitting, but for TALL and outsize fittings too! In a variety of delightful new colours. Hip sizes from 36" to 43½".

Berkertex introduces, for the first time, fittings for the taller woman: Height 5 ft. 7 ins. to 6 ft. Price 51/5d.

51/5d. Outsize to 48" hips 59/2d.
(11 coupons)

UTILITY CAN BE INDIVIDUAL

Unusual sizes now included.

Autumn Utility Styles which have just been released show beyond doubt that Utility and attractive dress designs can and do go hand in hand. In fact, it seems that Utility means a new high standard of fine styling, never before possible at moderate prices.

CAVENDISH HOUSE

are now displaying a selection of Berkertex Utility dresses designed by Norman Hartnell. Individuality is not only the keynote of the styling of these charming models. It is also apparent in the sizes in which they are available. No longer need the tall or outsize woman dismiss these new dresses from her thoughts with a regretful "not for me," for her needs are realised and now fully catered for.

Manufacturers were not keen; the take-up of templates only averaged about one to each designated firm. However, the scheme had the desired effect in that women became far more open to the idea of wearing Utility.

In mid-October, Utility dresses designed by the Queen's dressmaker, Norman Hartnell, went on display. The **Gloucestershire Echo** commented: *'If wartime has any blessings to bestow, perhaps one of these is that a woman can wear a dress bought for a very modest sum. Confessing to her friends that Norman Hartnell actually designed it.'*

ABOVE While not being part of the original couturier scheme, Norman Hartnell produced many Utility designs, including this one from November 1942.

Utility Furs

At the end of July 1942 the press reported that Utility fur coats might soon become available . This raised a few eyebrows. A fur coat was the epitome of luxury and seemed to have no place in a scheme which was all about producing affordable clothes.

The **Aberdeen Journal** reported that *'Talks are now going on between the Board of Trade and the fur industry to decide on what skins shall be incorporated in the Utility coat. It is expected that both pony fur and coney-skin will be the materials decided upon. Imports of fur have completely ceased since war began and only domestic skins are available for the making of coats.'*

However, it was not until November 1944 that it was announced that inexpensive fur garments would be added to the Utility range, mostly made of rabbit fur or sheepskin. The **Gloucester Journal** commented that *'Utility fur coats will be made of "home-grown" skins but will be far from recognised as such for it is possible to treat rabbit-skin so that it is almost indistinguishable from more precious pelts such as seal-skin, ocelot, musquash, summer ermine and chinchilla.'* The **Dundee Courier** predicted that *'Only the cheapest will be rabbit skin. Others will be really first-class dyed lamb and sheepskin.'*

The Board announced that Utility furs would include women's coats, jackets, boleros and capes, and men's waistcoats made from a variety of skins. In February

ABOVE 'Just Arrived' — a Utility fur advert from March 1945. Utility was supposed to supply affordable clothes for the working classes — many were understandably surprised at the provision of a coat costing £30.

OPPOSITE PAGE Full-length utility fur coat. People were surprised when furs were added to the scheme in late 1944; at up to £30 a coat such as this hardly came under the heading of 'affordable clothing', but in fact their inclusion was in an effort to boost the British fur trade.

ABOVE AND OPPOSITE PAGE Expensive looking furs like this were achieved by the artful dyeing of domestic furs, such as rabbit, sheepskin and fox. The finished article could be, from a distance, most deceptive.

1945 it announced that there were to be 18 lines of garments; the furs used, in ascending order of cost, would be sheepskin, rabbit, antelope, red fox, lamb, hair seal, jackal, mole, fitch, genet, opossum and wallaby. Prices would range from £9 to £27, according to the fur.

One problem was that furs were deemed luxury goods and so subject to 100 per cent purchase tax, whereas Utility goods were tax-exempt. In March Captain Charles Waterhouse, Parliamentary Secretary to the Board of Trade, proposed cutting purchase tax on Utility furs to 16 per cent. Some MPs were unhappy as this established a precedent of tax on Utility goods. Waterhouse countered that *'the reason that it does bear a tax, in distinction to the ordinary man's overcoat…is the fact that this is a much more expensive coat.'* Others argued that a fur coat had no place in a scheme for inexpensive clothing. Waterhouse explained that part of the idea was

D. M. Brown's
for
FINE FURS

A Word of Advice . . .

£29 : 18 : 6

MILLINERY

£2 : 13 : 11

D. M. BROWN, Ltd., High St., Dundee

ABOVE A full-length fur coat from
October 1946.

'to help the fur trade over a particularly difficult
period'. Rationing, purchase tax and the
disruption of international trade had severely
weakened Britain's fur trade. Now, with the
end of the war in sight, the Government
wanted to 'prime the pump' to prepare the fur
trade for post-war commerce.

The following day the **Gloucester Journal**
carried the news that *'The first of the Utility fur
coats are now on sale. Styles are pleasingly
varied and both material and workmanship
are good. The top price is £29 18s 6d –
with 15% extra for outsizes – for full
length coats, 43 ins long, lined
throughout, and made in genet,
wallaby, or beaver lamb fur. The same*
*length coats in musquash or dark antelope fur are offered at £19 19s.
One of these coats had sleeves and collar of beaver lamb. A beaver lamb
coat had vertical stripes shading from brown to
grey. The number of coupons required is 18.*

*'In jigger coats, beginning with those in
antelope fur at £15 10s 11d, prices range up
to £24 0s 6d for beaver lamb, grey lamb and
other furs. These require 12 coupons.*

*'Capes in natural and dyed fox are priced
at £19 and in moleskin and skunk-opossum at
£12 and £12 12s for three coupons. Fox, in
some cases, is dyed black and silvered, or
treated to imitate the cross and blue varieties,
or dyed a deep brown.'*

UTILITY
Fur Capes

Large consignment purchased in
London this week. Newest styles,
and all made from the best skins.
Brown Baby Seal Lamb. Price
£11.10.9.

Dyed Scotch Moleskins, £12.12.6.
£15.15.6 and £16 5/-.
Sable Dyed Genet, £13.13.6.
Black Fox, £15.
Phantom Beaver Coney. Prices
£15.15.9 and £18.
Cross Fox Dyed Fox Skins, Price
£18 18/-.
Rich Brown Fox Cape, as sketch,
Price £18 18/-.

(13 coupons.)

Fur Salon—First Floor.

Smiths

1-9 Murraygate, Dundee.
Phone 5041/2.

ABOVE Just in time for peace, this fur cape
advertisement dates from May 1945.

In late October 1949 the **Evening
Telegraph** reported, *'New furs come into the
Utility range this season, foremost amongst
them being Scottish moleskin and mink marmot. Dyed squirrel, worked like ermine, is
found now in the Utility range in all the soft browns that look so well in this fur.'* In mid-
November the **Gloucester Journal** announced that *'fur coats and fur hats for children
in the Utility ranges are coming along. Very few fur coats for children have been made in*

ABOVE Ladies' utility gauntlets. Made of leather and fur (probably rabbit). Fur was hardly the cheaper end of clothing which utility was meant to be, but in late 1944, the Board of trade included fur in the scheme to give the hard-pressed British fur business a boost.

recent years, the high rate of purchase tax on them made them too expensive to be economical. The new Utility coats will carry a much lower rate of tax.'

One year later, the **Sunday Post** declared that 'Many women – from young girls to their grannies – are plumping for fur rather than tweed or cloth coats. Eight out of ten have bought Utility fur coats. They wanted to get in before the price went up. And they managed – for this weekend prices have gone up 15%.'

IT'S STOCKIN'S——WOT'S
MY "BLUE PENCIL" HEADACHE!

Stockings

Obtaining stockings became a real problem for women under rationing. A Board exhibition, 'Count Your Coupons', informed visitors in 1942 that *'Before the war, a woman bought 13 pairs of silk stockings a year. In the first year of rationing, she bought about seven pairs.'* As rationing tightened, most would be lucky if they had sufficient coupons for three pairs a year. Under such conditions, stockings needed to last.

In October 1941 the **Nottingham Evening Post** reported that *'Only women in the services may be able to wear shapely, fully-fashioned stockings [shaped to the leg] soon. For the rest a new kind of stocking – unshaped and with no seam up the back – is likely to be introduced. Manufacturers have been experimenting with these utility stockings, and if Board of Trade experts approve them, big scale production will start and the stockings will sell at controlled prices within the reach of everybody. They can be made very quickly and by unskilled labour.'*

At the end of November, Sir Andrew Duncan informed Parliament: *'The Limitation of Supplies Orders make special provision for the supply of stockings of a utility character'.* The **Western Times** reported, *'...the Government is bringing out utility ranges in stockings which they say will wear well, and include rayon at 2s 1d to 2s 7d a pair, also a mixture of rayon and cotton at the same price, as well as hard-wearing lisle.'*

Unlike Utility textiles in general, where only the cloth had to be made to tight specifications while the garments themselves were left to the choice of the designers (and the austerity provisions), certain Utility items, including hosiery, corsetry and knitted goods, were also subject to design specifications.

In February 1942 Utility stockings were beginning to appear on the market. The **Yorkshire Post** and **Leeds Mercury** commented: *'If the Utility stockings wear well they will solve the vexed wartime stocking problem, although naturally they cannot compare with the fashioned pure silk of peace days. As an emergency measure, however, they are far better than might have been expected. Unfashioned, with a mock seam, they have a smooth, dull finish, and the range of colours from pale suntan shades through half a dozen neutral beiges to the deeper tones are excellent.'*

OPPOSITE PAGE Stockings were 'coupon-expensive' – a woman's woollen or fully-fashioned stockings required a precious 3 coupons a pair. The first solution was the use of leg make-up, but a general shortage of cosmetics soon put a stop to that idea. Utility stockings were an attempt at a solution, but were plagued with problems.

On 17 January 1943 it was announced that *'Fully-fashioned Utility stockings in four colours will be on sale in the spring. Some will be of rayon, others lisle. Majority will be seamless, but there will be a fair proportion of fully-fashioned pairs. Colours will be mist beige, vogue, Newmarket and dryad.'*

Utility stockings were plagued by problems, mostly of fit and durability. On 26 February 1943 the **Aberdeen Journal** reported that *'Following the many complaints that the Utility rayon hosiery tends to ladder easily and wear badly, the board of trade has introduced new specifications. Some of the lower grades have been eliminated and an extra allocation of cotton yard has been secured to strengthen heels and toes. Prices will be unchanged.'* A fortnight later, the **Gloucester Journal** had more details: *'It is promised that the new stocking will be thicker, stronger and more shapely when seamless, that it will be at least 29 inches in length, and…it will be mostly made of cotton and rayon mixtures. These stockings, it is declared, will be better than some pre-war kinds.'*

When Hugh Dalton was quizzed on their quality, he replied, *'I have stopped the production of one of the utility specifications which has proved unsatisfactory, and I am having others revised. In addition, I shall shortly require each manufacturer to apply an identification mark to all utility knitted goods made by him.'*

On 2 April 1944 the **Sunday Post** reported that the *'First Utility seamless stockings in the new Leap Year shade will be on sale next week. A sandy skin tone, the new colour is the palest yet used for Utility stockings.'* On 26 June the **Gloucester Journal** assessed *'the new 3s-a-pair Utility stockings which the Board of Trade hope will answer all complaints.'* Its verdict – *'The new stocking is not beautiful but it is strong.'*

ABOVE Pure Silk and Bemberg' utility stockings. Bemberg was a form of viscose, sometimes called artificial, or 'art' silk.

In December 1944 the **Gloucester Journal** informed its readers that *'According to a Board of Trade official, the "731" stocking has become a best-seller. Supplies have been increased without satisfying the demand. The durability tests carried out by experts have been fully borne out in public use. The "731" stockings are not, of course, fully-fashioned, but only one fifth of the stockings produced today are fully-fashioned'* The 731 designation referred to the manufacturing specification, of which there were many variations; the 731 proved to be one of the most hard-wearing.

On 24 January 1946 the **Evening Telegraph** gave its female readers the long-awaited news that *'Nylon stockings – 300,000 pairs of them a week – will be on the market by June. There will be both fully-fashioned and seamless stockings in a variety of colours. But they will all be in the Utility range as that is the only way in which prices can be controlled.'* On 31 August the **Gloucester Journal** stated that *'Before Christmas it is now definitely expected that Utility nylon stockings will begin to appear at prices to suit everyone. Two grades are being manufactured, one with cotton tops and feet and the other an all-nylon stocking. The cotton-top stockings will probably sell at 9s*

Whenever I see hands in a stocking I think : "Ah—

Aristoc!"

Sigh no more, lady. Both you and we look forward to the day when there will be a more generous supply of your favourite stockings. Meanwhile we are making *Aristoc Utility* in attractive shades. Supplies are limited but fair shares are distributed to all Aristoc dealers.

FINE GAUGE FULL-FASHIONED STOCKINGS

ABOVE Like many wartime advertisements, this one from June 1945 looks forward to a time of plenty.

6d a pair. At first there will be only small quantities of all-nylon stockings supplied to the shops and these will sell at about 10s 6d a pair.' In October Utility stocking specifications and prices for them were announced by the Board. There would be five fully-fashioned (two all-nylon), and two 'no-seam' types. Maximum retail prices were to range between 8s 3d and 9s 10d per pair for fully fashioned and 6s 11d for seamless.

By mid-March 1947 the **Gloucester Journal** reported that Utility silk stockings were due to arrive in two to three weeks' time. *'The first batch will be made from Italian yarn and will cost 7s 6d a pair. Both fully-fashioned and mock-fashioned Utility stockings are being made in a range of colours.'*

At the beginning of January 1950 it was announced that from April all the Utility stocking specifications were to be replaced by three broad ones.

Foundation Garments

Another main area of complaint was Utility corsetry. In January 1942 the Board set maximum prices ranging from 8s 1d to 24s 2d for corselets and lace-front corsets, 5s 9d to 24s 2d for wrap-around and back-lace corsets, 4s 6d to 8s 1d for suspender belts, and 3s to 8s 1d for ordinary brassieres.

By 1943 scarcity of rubber meant that controls were introduced for elastic, which could only be used for corsets and knickers, and even then only in short lengths. In June the **Gloucester Journal** remarked that *'Other complaints made about Utility goods concern corsets…some corsets take on the shape of the body instead of giving the body shape. Bad corsets are said to be the result of rubber and steel shortages.'* Six months later things had not improved; the paper noted: *'They are said to give no "support" and, as a result, are bad for health, especially for elderly*

ABOVE Women's underwear was amongst the first utility items.

women who may have to stand at factory benches, behind counters, and in queues. It seems there is not enough steel used in the corset. It is complained that often after a week's wear Utility corsets "collapse like concertinas". The suspenders, it is said, being

OPPOSITE PAGE Women's utility vest. Central heating in private homes was very rare; what with that, fuel shortages, and later, rationing, it was important to dress up well, especially in the winter. See the model on the left of the photograph on page 32.

LEFT Like hosiery, items of corsetry were subject to design specifications, but rubber shortages meant they were often not up to the task demanded of them.

large and rigid, pull holes in stockings and "usually snap off in a fortnight".' In the week before Christmas the paper had better news: *'Reinforced Utility corsets, strengthened with hardened steel, will soon be going into production.'*

At the end of February 1944 the **Dundee Courier** reported on a new schedule of Utility corsets. *'For women who take medium sizes there will be Utility corsets made of particularly hard-wearing cloths which have up to now been used only in the manufacture of outsizes, where extra support was needed. Utility hookside corsets in smaller sizes may now be manufactured in styles using the same amount of elastic and metal bone fastenings as are used in larger sizes.'*

ABOVE Men's or youth's utility trunks. In the latter part of the war such elastic waistbands were banned.

RIGHT Women's utility 'bloomers'; in April 1942 such embroidery was banned.

FACTS AND FIGURES

Austerity days are here. It's a hard fact. But in the post-war world, C.B. Foundations will meet every demand for fashionable figures. Even if you *do* have difficulty in obtaining C.B. Corsets and Brassieres whilst the war is on, you will have your reward in the inimitable cut and style which C.B. always provides

CB
CORSETRY

CHARLES BAYER & CO. (1931) LTD., LOWER BRISTOL ROAD, BATH

ABOVE Early utility brassieres such as this were a cause of much complaint. A lack of elastic, and strong materials in their manufacture meant they gave little support, especially for larger busts. The Board of Trade responded with improved specifications.

RIGHT An advert for Meridian utility 'pantees', from September 1944, claiming to be "as good as peacetime".

However, the supply of the sort of steel needed was still very limited, and so, therefore, were the corsets.

In August 1944 new Utility corsets were announced. The **Gloucester Journal** informed its readers that they were *'nothing like pre-war quality although they are better than anything we have seen since the war.'* Less than a week later the Board announced that, from September, corset manufacturers could use the strongest Utility cloths previously used only for size 28 inches upwards, in corsets of all sizes. Also the making of outsize corsets from the lightest Utility cloths would be prohibited, and the amount of elastic in Utility brassieres

When it comes to "Utility"—and good as your peace-time Meridian was, it cannot last for ever—then you cannot do better than rely on "Utility Wear by Meridian," because coupons are precious. This Meridian *PANTEE* is only 2 coupons.

J. B. LEWIS & SONS LTD., Nottingham.   Estd. 1815.   Suppliers to the Wholesale Trade

increased. On 28 October the **Gloucester Journal** noted that *'the first stocks of steel-standard corsets are to become almost immediately available in the shops',* although only in limited numbers.

In February 1945 the Board announced that it was lifting restrictions on the use of metal in all Utility corsets and of double body cloth in brassieres. In November, it allowed the industry to recommence the manufacture of synthetic

G. L. WILSON

CORSET WEEK

" J.B.,"   " TWILFIT,"
" BERLEI,"   " COURT
ROYAL " in Corselettes,
Underbelt, Front Lace, Back
Lace, etc.
ALL super Utility or General
Numbers.

BRASSIERES

" BERLEI," " TWILFIT,"
and " GOTHIC." Assorted
from Short to Deep Shapes.

Fittings by appointment.

" The Corner," Dundee

LEFT A February 1948 advertisement for super Utility corsets. Super Utility was a response to people's rejection of the cheaper grade of Utility garment, and denoted a new top-grade of Utility. Super Utility numbers began with an X.

LEFT Boys utility vest, stamped on the front. Many items of wool-type underwear bore such stamps.

rubber suspender collets (the button-type piece which holds the stocking), much to the relief of women who reported that Utility suspenders either failed to keep stockings up, or laddered them.

In the week before Christmas the Board extended the scheme for Utility corsets and brassieres; manufacturers would now produce 16 models instead of eight. Most of the extra models were of the more expensive 'super Utility' type. A super Utility laced-back corset with belt cost 21s, while the old improved Utility price was 17s 9d, and the ordinary Utility price was 13s 3d. Deep brassieres, previously costing 4s 10d and 6s 1d, now included a super Utility model costing up to 7s 6d. The Board also authorised a new cloth, originally woven for parachutes, to be used for brassieres and sections of corselettes.

In late February 1946 the production of roll-on corsets, that had not been manufactured for nearly four years, was resumed; maximum prices were to be 5s 6d for a one-way stretch garment, and 7s 5d for a two-way stretch garment.

RIGHT A Twilfit advert from Christmas 1944.

AN *Announcement*

THE "Twilfit" tradition of quality has not changed during the War. We are still putting into our garments the very best materials and workmanship obtainable, and in the days that follow the war your "Twilfit" Corset will continue to give that graceful line that makes for figure beauty.

Meanwhile your favourite model may be unobtainable, but you will find in our present range a Utility number incorporating all your requirements.

Twilfit Regd. *Corsetry*

LEETHEMS (TWILFIT) LTD., PORTSMOUTH

OPPOSITE PAGE Children's short utility socks. As with men's socks, children's socks were almost all of the ankle-sock type, to save on scarce materials. The H prefix (right) denoted knitted items and included socks, stockings, underwear, bathing costumes and pullovers.

ALL WOOL
H67A 664 MHP
SHRINK RESIST'NG

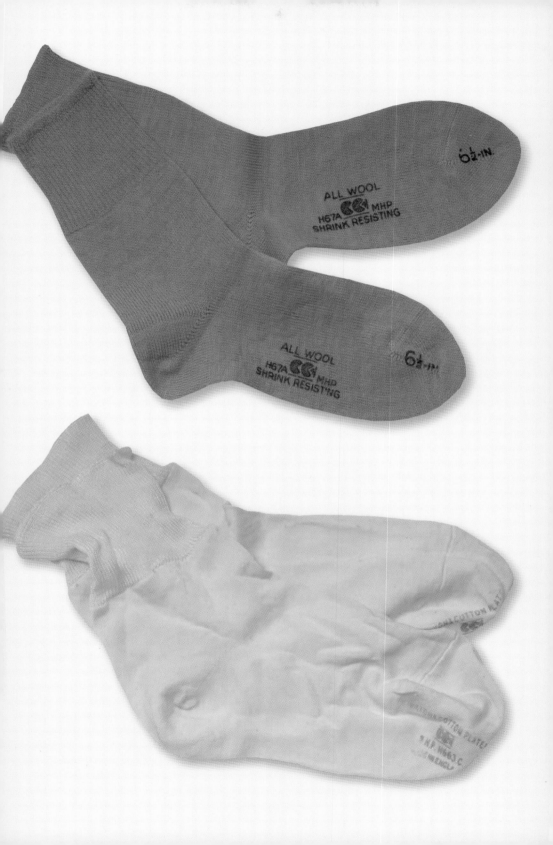

ALL WOOL
H67A ⟨⟨⟨⟩⟩ MHP
SHRINK RESISTING

6½-IN.

ALL WOOL
H67A ⟨⟨⟨⟩⟩ MHP
SHRINK RESIST'NG

6½-IN.

Utility in Operation
July 1942 to November 1945

In the House of Commons, on 23 July 1942, Hugh Dalton announced that *'Utility clothing now amounts to about 70 or 80 per cent of the total civilian production.'* However, non-Utility clothing was not free from regulation; two days later the **Evening Telegraph** reported that *'The Board of Trade have also fixed maximum prices for all cloth, clothing, household textiles, and bedding, both within the Utility range and outside it. Non-utility goods already in the shops are subject to the new Orders, which forbid manufacturers to charge higher prices than those charged on June 30 last.'* Now all clothing was price-controlled.

On 3 August, one month earlier than originally announced, Utility clothing, and Utility cloth for making into garments, joined Utility footwear in becoming exempt from purchase tax. Gloves were controlled from September by new directives for the production of Utility leather gloves, and a smaller number of Utility cotton fabric and Astrakhan gloves – the latter reserved for children.

In June 1943 braces were added to the Utility scheme, due to the rubber shortage. The **Nottingham Evening Post** informed its readers that *'They*

OPPOSITE PAGE AND ABOVE Pretty utility two piece suit. Its very basic cut is lifted by the diagonal art deco-style seam across the bodice, finishing in a rather jazzy feature at the bustline. Another feature is the way the belt disappeared at the front, tying at the back.

It's a dream... it's HARELLA

LEFT Two women's Utility overcoats, September 1943.

OPPOSITE PAGE Boy's utility shirt, conforming to austerity rules, it has no pocket, and opens at the neck only.

will be made of soft leather or webbing, but no elastic or rubber. Prices to the public will vary from 2s to 3s 6d.' Of course, there's an obvious flaw in braces with no elastic, and it soon showed; as this letter to the **Sunday Post** illustrates. *'Scene – the bowling green. Time –Saturday afternoon. I had the honour of throwing the first bowl. I drew back the bowl and bent down.*

PICK THE GARMENT WITH THIS LABEL

THIS IS PICK Brand KNITWEAR

Pick Utility Pull-
overs, Slipovers,
Jerseys for men,
women & children

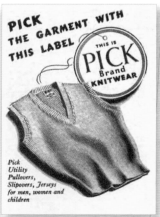

PICK THE GARMENT WITH THIS LABEL

THIS IS PICK Brand KNITWEAR

Pick
Utility
Pullovers,
Slipovers, Jerseys
for men, women and
children

PICK the garment with this label

THIS IS A PICK Brand GARMENT

Ask for Pick Utility Knitwear: Cardigans,
Pullovers, Slipovers for men and boys.
Jerseys for boys and girls.
Made by J. Pick and Sons Ltd., Leicester

ABOVE AND RIGHT These Pick advertisements from 1942 to 1945 illustrate a good selection of the types of Utility knitwear available.

A Harella Utility overcoat and suit, September 1943. Photographer, Norman Parkinson.

Then snap went my Utility braces. First time on, and now only fit for salvage!'

By July an unexpected effect of rationing was becoming apparent. Dalton was asked in the Commons *'whether he is aware that owing to the fact that a coupon is equally valid in purchasing a low-priced or an expensive article, holders are refusing to purchase other than the most expensive types of boots, shoes and clothing, leaving heavy unsold stocks in the hands of wholesalers and retailers?'*

What happened next demonstrated the ability of the Board's clothing schemes to respond to changes in supply and demand. In mid-August it was announced that, from September, men's three-piece suits costing under 55s 3d and women's costumes priced at less than 62s 2d would be among items of the cheapest grade Utility clothing that would need fewer coupons – 20 coupons instead of 26, and 12 instead of 18 respectively. The **Sunday Post** responded, *'Will this do any good? No! Women refuse to part with valued coupons for shoddy articles.'*

In mid-November the Ministry of Supply announced that it was purchasing thousands of articles of clothing to form a stock for clothing the populations of occupied Europe. *'This will be Utility clothing and of inferior quality.'*

In February 1944 the high price of women's hats was discussed in Parliament. Dalton said, *'I have given anxious thought to this difficult problem, but there is infinite*

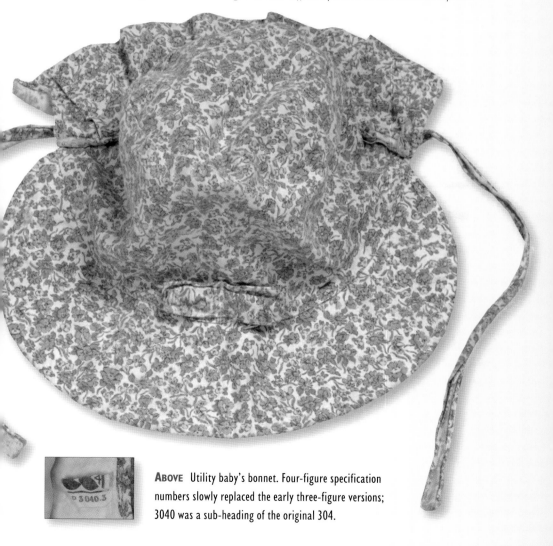

ABOVE Utility baby's bonnet. Four-figure specification numbers slowly replaced the early three-figure versions; 3040 was a sub-heading of the original 304.

THE AUSTERITY CHILD

has had to forgo so many of the delightful health garments which in peace time comprised our Kamella range.

But now the return of our Utility Baby Bags will be welcomed by mothers everywhere.

Supplies of these and other Kamella utility garments are, of course, very restricted, but it pays to look out for Kamella quality.

KAMELLA

KAMELLA LIMITED
BRADFORD

LEFT Utility encompassed children's and babies' wear, such as this 'baby bag' that dates from December 1944.

BELOW Baby's utility dress or christening dress. Although made without frills or embroidery, there was nothing to stop them being added after purchase.

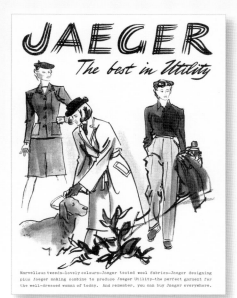

Marvellous tweeds—lovely colours—Jaeger tested wool fabrics—Jaeger designing plus Jaeger making combine to produce Jaeger Utility—the perfect garment for the well-dressed woman of today. And remember, you can buy Jaeger everywhere.

LEFT Many leading makers, such as Burton's, Marks and Spencer and Jaeger, produced Utility wear; these examples date from September 1943.

variety in women's hats and I am very doubtful whether a Utility model, even at a fixed price, would be welcome.' A few days later, it was the turn of men's socks, Dalton being asked if he was aware that the short-leg Utility socks were practically unsaleable. He replied, *'Some millions of pairs of these socks are being sold each month. That is not what I should call being practically unsaleable.'* One month later he promised to consider production of a Utility handbag at a reasonable price; however, *'with the present shortage of leather any such handbag would have to be made of other material.' In December he dropped the idea.*

Early in April maximum prices for children's Utility clothes were announced for the first time, the system to come into operation from 1 July. However, the list did not include prices for hosiery and footwear, for which there were separate regulations. The range, it was announced, would be wide, with new clothes to be marked 'C.P.', indicating that they were subject to ceiling prices. In the event, this measure was delayed until mid-August.

RIGHT A Harella Utility top-coat from October 1942.

It's a dream it's HARELLA

Exhibition of combined operations by Harella — a treasure of a utility coat, light as cloud, warm as sunshine and flattering as a compliment, in fleecy dove-beige Alpaca mixture, fully lined crepe, 102/10d : combined with a tailored utility suit of pure West of England wool (in many colourful checks) 92/10d. See both, together with many other triumphant Harella 'couples' at any good fashion store; or if in any difficulty write to the Harella Showrooms, 243 Regent Street, London, W.1. (Wholesale only.)

Post-War Utility

On 15 February 1943 Sir Thomas Barlow, Director-General of Civilian Clothing, asked manufacturers to consider whether the Utility schemes should be continued after the war. Rationing and Utility were deemed wartime necessities, and the idea that either might continue post-war came as a shock to some people.

On 23 March 1945, with the end of the war in sight, the BBC broadcast a discussion on 'Utility production in Peacetime'. The war had made people concentrate on the sort of post-war Britain for which they were fighting. For many on the political right, peace promised a return to free trade and the casting-off of 'war socialism'. For the left it meant continued social provision, implementation of the Beveridge Report, public ownership, and the establishment of the National Health Service.

In April, Hugh Dalton informed Parliament that *'the future of the Utility Clothing scheme after the war has not yet been decided.'*

On 5 July 1945, with Germany defeated and the war against Japan

" The Government should celebrate victory by passing an Act expunging the words utility and queue from the English language."

ABOVE A cartoon from June 1946. Like rationing, Utility was seen by some as a necessary 'evil' in wartime that would disappear shortly after the war was over.

drawing to a close, the people got to choose between the two political philosophies in a General Election. The result was an unexpected Labour landslide victory: Clement Attlee became Prime Minister with a majority of 145 seats.

OPPOSITE PAGE A super-utility men's three-piece suit. At 5 coupons, a waistcoat was something of a luxury under rationing; meant men often opted to replace it with a hand-knitted sweater, made using wool recycled by taking down older items of knitwear.

The rejection of the cheapest of the three Utility grades by the general public signalled a move to the dearer end of the range. A new fourth grade, positioned above the old top grade, was envisaged, and it was to be called 'Super Utility'. On the night of Labour's victory, the Board announced details of ceiling prices for the new Super Utility clothing. Men's ready-made suits would cost up to £8 15s 5d, compared with £6 1s 3d previously. Women's costumes would be up to £6 2s 2d ready-made and £7 10s 9d made to measure as against £5 2s 2d and £5 12s 3d respectively.

As higher-grade Utility garments with higher maximum prices were introduced, it made sense to do the same with non-Utility clothing. In November 1945 these details were announced in Parliament: *'Overcoat, raincoat, mackintosh, or like garment, including any coat, cape or cloak, more than 28ins in length, £20. Wool, or part wool, costume, consisting of skirt and tailored or fully-lined jacket, £20 — not being both tailored with fully-lined jacket or cardigan, £17 11s. Costume not made wholly or mainly of wool cloth, consisting of skirt and jacket or cardigan, £14 8s. Dress of wool or part-wool cloth — including pinafore dress and two-piece dress — housecoat, dressing gown, or costume, other than as described in the preceding paragraphs, £15 15s. Skirt,*

including divided shirt – or slacks, £6. Jacket, blazer, cardigan, waistcoat bolero, or like garment, including any coat, cape or cloak not more than 28ins in length, wool or part wool, £11 11s; not made wholly or mainly of wool cloth, £8 8s. Blouse or jumper, £5.'

The **Western Morning News** reported that *'The new control will not apply to retail prices before March 1. Arrangements are being made for a distinguishing mark to be used eventually to indicate which garments will qualify for the higher range of prices.'*

In February 1946, the **Daily Mirror** reported a 25 per cent increase in the production of elastic. *'This will all go into higher grades of super-Utility corsets, elastic braces, suspenders and garters.'* Towards the end of March the Board announced that from April elastic could be used without restriction in the manufacture of underwear, outerwear, hose, men's garters and suspenders. Utility braces with elastic inserts or with elastic cord ends could also be manufactured. Surprisingly, three years later the **Derby Evening Telegraph** revealed that *'Seven out of ten men are going about wearing braces that are frayed and bedraggled. They got so used to "won't stretch" Service braces and Utility civilian types during the war that many of them won't bother to buy the springy, artistic 1949 creations now in the shops.'*

OPPOSITE PAGE AND ABOVE Woman's short coat or housecoat. It's late date is shown by the four-figure specification number, and by the pattern, which is very 1950s; the spiralling lines and the colours, especially the pastel green and red, are very evocative of the period.

Women and their
Underwear

PRE-WAR—more than a million regular wearers knew and appreciated the finer qualities of *Vedonis* —and they *insisted* upon having *Vedonis*. TO-DAY — they and other discerning women choose the 'next best '— Vedoknit — knowing full well it is top grade 'utility' —the best to be had to-day.

Vedoknit
'Utility' Underwear made by *Vedonis*

LEFT This advertisement, from December 1945, makes interesting reading; while it does not attain pre-war standards, top grade Utility is 'the best to be had to-day'.

In April 1946 came the Budget, and the news that purchase tax was to stay. In the Commons, some MPs, especially Conservatives, complained that it had been introduced specifically as a war tax. Lt-Commander Gurney Braithwaite (Holderness) declared, '…*it is a grossly unfair tax upon the fair sex, who might look forward, as austerity is relieved, to blossoming forth in those changes of apparel so dear to their hearts. They will find that this tax presses harshly on many of the things they would like to have. Let no one imagine that the ladies of this country are going to content themselves with utility clothing for a moment longer than is necessary.*'

At the end of April the **Dundee Courier** commented on super-Utility clothes: '*A very few tailors are anxious to make these garments, and certainly few people want to wear them. The very word Utility makes them shiver. Such garments are looked upon as a waste both of time and coupons.*' Three weeks later the **Sunday Post** took a different line: '*Is it worthwhile buying utility clothes now that prices are going up? Take it from me – even if the prices of suits go up by £3, you're getting better value for money compared to non-Utility stuff. Here's a tip – if you decide on Utility buy the best you can afford. The higher the price the better the bargain!*' That month the **Gloucester Journal** joined the debate. '*Wartime Utility fashions are now in the process of passing and during the next few months [will be] replaced by peacetime Utility, which, in turn, should lose any particular identity from other clothes – perhaps before the end of the autumn. The announcement of a revision in Utility prices heralds a greater variety in the ways of making and the signs are that the raising of the maximum prices is to allow this to be done. Following the freedom from austerity restrictions it marks another stage in the direction of a pre-war state of affairs in clothing.*'

In mid-1946 the cost-plus control was removed from Utility knitted goods, and it was replaced by a system of cash maximum prices only, to be fixed rather lower than ceiling prices would have been under the old system.

OPPOSITE PAGE AND RIGHT Super-utility women's jacket from a suit, 1948. The registration mark tells all; the X is super-utility (from January 1948), the three-figure number is pre-November 1948, and the /1 shows that it is part of a multiple-piece set.

ABOVE AND LEFT The 'dinner plate' or 'double elevens' label. There has been much controversy over its meaning, but, simply, it signified the non-utility equivalent of super-utility, the top of the price range for non-utility garments. Its quality is obvious in this jacket.

LEFT A customer examines a woollen Utility frock requiring 11 coupons in a department store in London's West End. One of the great advantages of the rationing system was that unpopular goods could be 'coupon-reduced' to clear stocks or, as in this case, price-reduced.

In August Ellis Smith, Parliamentary Secretary to the Board of Trade, informed the Commons that *'Discussions are being renewed with the various interests to settle conditions for the removal of the style restrictions on women's and children's outerwear and underwear at a convenient date early next year.'*

At the end of August it was reported that wedding dresses, hitherto almost unobtainable, might reappear as Utility articles. In addition, six new Utility fabrics were shortly to be in the shops.

In November 1946 the **Gloucester Journal** reported that *'A change in the price control on women's costumes is to be made at the end of the year when present ceiling prices – £20 for coat or costume – will apply only to women's and maids' non-Utility clothing which bears the mark "11011".'*

'For garments not so marked, not more than the following "ceiling" prices may be charged: coats or tailored costumes, £14; untailored costumes, nine and a half guineas, and, if wool, £12 1s 0d, dresses, eight guineas, and, if wool, ten guineas; four guineas is the limit for skirts, slacks, blouses or boleros; jackets over 16ins long, five and a half guineas and, if wool, seven and a half guineas; dress and tailored jackets, wool, £20 6s 0d.' This mark has become known (erroneously) as 'double Utility', or the 'dinner plate mark'.

In the same month the Board allowed men's caps to be made from Utility cloth, thus hugely increasing their availability.

At this time Utility was beginning to get a bad name because of some shoddy suppliers. The **Daily Mirror** reported: *'No-name firms, who count on getting out with the gold when that time comes, are those who give Utility a bad name. They skimp the cloth, fail to shrink it beforehand or to match the pattern carefully in a weave like herringbone or check. They cut too many coats at once, so that they lose in fit and exactness.*

Modern
Maternity

Be sure to see the
Special Display of
Maternity Gowns
in our Windows and   FIRST
Gown Salon . . . . .   FLOOR

From our Collection of Utility Rayon
Maternity Gowns, the sketch depicts
one in Paisley design. . . . Other
styles are available in Self and Printed
Rayon. . . . . Also Smock Suits.
Price 57/11   7 Coupons

Falconers   UNION STREET
                   ABERDEEN

LEFT The Utility scheme encompassed almost all types of clothing, including maternity wear. This example is from April 1947.

They sling in any old lining, any old how. (Linings are scarce, I know, but a conscientious firm will give you a telling contrast if not a perfect match.) They try to "press" the coat after the lining has gone in, instead of before, which is naturally much less thorough. They use coarse stitching and do not care if it's not quite straight. They are not "choosey" about the quality of cloth. Perhaps they cannot be. It's the good coat-maker who gets the best from the good cloth-maker.'

However, the paper argued that, with the price of non-Utility clothing rocketing, the best of Utility was a great bargain – *'So that's why I shall buy Utility – and take out the CC41 label, the only thing that really gives it away. It's the other label – the name of the firm who made or sold me my coat that really matters.'*

This was a telling reversal of the earlier practice of removing the label to sell the item for more than the controlled price – now you took it out to make people think you paid more for it.

In late January 1947 Stafford Cripps, the President of the Board of Trade, informed the Commons that 84 per cent of woollen clothing fabric manufactured for the home market was Utility. In June, the government subsidy on household textiles, which varied from 20 per cent to 60 per cent of the manufacturers' ceiling price, was removed, while the subsidy on apparel cloths and handkerchief cloths was removed in January 1948. These measures covered more than 40 per cent of the manufacturers' ceiling prices. Prices inevitably rose. During May Phil Piratin, a Communist Party of Great Britain MP, referred in the House of Commons to *'the withdrawal of the subsidies of £33 million on cloth, leather and furs which make up our clothing. In this evening's paper we read that immediately the cost of a woman's utility top price coat has gone up by 22s to 30s, and a man's suit has increased in price by 27s to 36s.'*

ABOVE A very classy Utility dress by Marldena gowns, a branch of the Marlbeck fashion company.

In January 1948, the distinguishing mark 'X' was introduced. It appeared, in addition to the Utility mark, on dearer Utility clothing made of cotton and cotton rayon mixture. The **Aberdeen Journal** commented: *'Once only convicts wore clothing with government marks on it. Now we all have to wear it. Under-garments as well as outer are adorned, not with broad arrows certainly, but with Utility marks, marks showing the grade of textile used, "O's" and dashes for the highest grade of cloth [IIOII], and now "X's" showing that it costs more than it used to. Add an extra ten minutes to the make-do-and-mend sessions for the cutting-off of all such labels; don't think about the time and labour involved in putting them on, not to mention thinking them out.'*

In September 1948 Harold Wilson replaced Stafford Cripps as President of the Board. In November he announced a new pricing method for Utility clothing. *'During the war, and for some time afterwards the price of most Utility clothing was governed by cost-plus, subject to ceiling prices. We have for some time been trying to find other effective means of control wherever possible.'* The result was the cash maximum prices system which had been introduced for knitted goods two years previously. At first, specifications for Utility items had been so vague that it was impossible to work out a general price for, say, a shirt. As a result a system of 'cost-plus' was employed, allowing a set percentage profit on top of the cost of garments, up to the maximum controlled price. Now, specifications for individual garments were very much tighter and so overall prices for many items could be set. This led to a labelling change; such items were no longer marked with the cloth specification number, but with the garment specification number. Wilson continued, *'Cost-plus has now been removed from men's, youths' and boys' Utility outerwear;*

UTILITY LABELS ABOVE Printed post-1948 4-figure. **OPPOSITE PAGE, TOP LEFT** Printed post-1948 super-utility. **BOTTOM LEFT** Dinner plate mark (see pages 110 and 111).
TOP RIGHT Printed early 3-figure number. **CENTRE RIGHT** Post 1948 woven lingerie label, two-piece set.
BOTTOM RIGHT Stamped mark for hosiery or knitted wool underwear.

CC41
X 3061/3
St Michael REGD
MADE IN GT. BRITAIN
5324/83
Size W.

CC41
206

CC41
Excelsior
1106/2

Caldaric

WEST OF ENGLAND
BY TUCKERS OF FROME

ALL WOOL
H67A CC41 MHD
SHRINK RESISTING

Utility waterproofs; Utility gaberdine raincoats, and women's Utility woven rayon underwear. I hope to make a similar change with other Utility garments in the near future.'

In the same month 'The Utility Cloth and Clothings Scheme' stated that 'the Utility scheme has been continued mainly as a means of keeping down prices and the cost of living and so lessening demands for wage increases which would lead to inflation.'

In mid-March 1949, the Aberdeen Journal commented that *'Growing dislike of the word Utility is leading to a ban on the name in many fashion circles. Two of the brightest stores in London have just rubbed out the description from their showrooms. They are using the phrase 'Moderate Income Clothes' or 'Budget Department' to embrace all cheaper good quality clothes.'* The concept of Utility was still valid, but the name was becoming devalued. The report continued, *'"The word Utility has outgrown its usefulness"; "It is getting a bad selling point," were opinions expressed by the trade yesterday.'* And most interesting of all, *'The Board of Trade view is*

ABOVE Even Utility could not ignore the new look. This Utility dress with matching bolero has a rather full, and definitely long, skirt, 1948.

that manufacturers should get together and agree on some other quality mark that will eventually take the place of Utility. An organisation to sponsor such a move is the British Standards Institution.'

On 14 March 1949, Wilson told Parliament, *'I should like to inform the House that I have today signed an Order ending completely the clothes rationing system. From tomorrow morning coupons will no longer be required for the purchase of any kind of clothing or textiles.'*

OPPOSITE PAGE Another very-1950s fabric. The colours; white, black and dark blue, and the pattern, are extremely reminiscent of cartoon backgrounds from the period, while the broad collar and longer skirt are both very much of their time.

The End of Utility

On the day after the end of clothes rationing, Wilson spoke again, this time to disappoint those who thought that the measure might also mean an end to Utility. Instead he announced that Utility clothing production was to be stepped up from 70 to 75 per cent of total output to 80 per cent (Utility footwear was already at 94 per cent). Further, price control would remain as long as was needed.

In his budget a few weeks later, the Chancellor, Stafford Cripps, disappointed many in the clothing trade by not including any purchase tax concessions. The general opinion in trade circles was that this would intensify the slump in the buying of non-Utility clothing, and increase the demand for tax-free Utility lines. In May the **Derby Daily Telegraph** noted that *'Utility pyjamas are in great demand because the prices are so reasonable – from 18s 6d for cotton printed – and the quality is good for the price. But once you leave the Utility range behind, prices are up to 50s and more – this great jump in prices also applies to Utility and non-Utility nightdresses.'*

LEFT An advertisement for the 'People on Sunday' newspaper from February 1950, showing how the Utility mark had become devalued in consumers' eyes.

At the end of July, Wilson announced a 5 per cent cut in the maximum prices of Utility clothing, footwear and domestic textiles, to take effect in September. Furs and fully-fashioned stockings were not included. The Independent Traders' Alliance responded that shopkeepers' profits would be cut by half; they would be compelled to sell only non-Utility goods to make a livelihood.

OPPOSITE PAGE Men's super-utility overcoat. Super-utility was the highest price range of utility clothing, and the quality of the coat is obvious. The material appears fine as opposed to scratchy, and the cut and finish appear to be good quality. Double-breasted jackets were banned for a time, but not overcoats.

ABOVE Slippers like these were brought into the Utility scheme from mid-1948.

TOP LEFT A very modern-looking Utility shoe from October 1949.

TOP RIGHT 'The new Utility shoes' from September 1948, the high heels showing the relaxation of the austerity provisions.

At the end of February 1950, the **People** newspaper ran an article which began: *'Millions of British women have for ten years looked on the Utility label as a talisman. In a period of shortage and rising prices, Utility has been the watchword for cheapness and quality but the famous label is now becoming a fraud. Utility goods are no longer sold at prices everyone can afford and for women's clothes above all the guarantee of quality that went with the Utility sign will soon be a mockery.*

'Utility prices have gone up and with some justification. Costs have soared – higher wages are being paid to the workers; raw materials are more expensive. But while costs have gone up, the standard of clothes has gone down – both in workmanship and in the quality of the materials.

RIGHT Another sign of easing austerity – men's long socks from February 1950. The H41 designation is their specification number, H being the prefix for knitted items.

BELOW Men's socks with the earlier specification L(wool)52 which became longer H numbers.

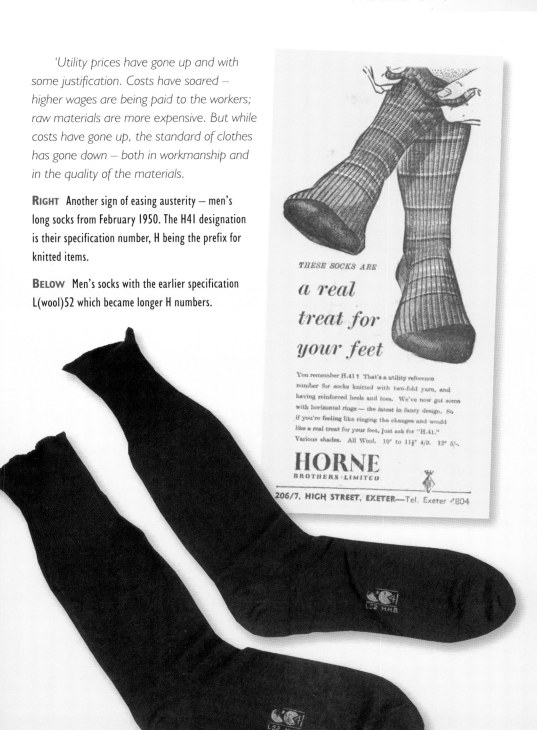

THESE SOCKS ARE

a real treat for your feet

You remember H.41 ? That's a utility reference number for socks knitted with two-fold yarn, and having reinforced heels and toes. We've now got some with horizontal rings — the latest in fancy design. So if you're feeling like ringing the changes and would like a real treat for your feet, just ask for "H.41." Various shades. All Wool. 10" to 11½" 4/9. 12" 5/-.

HORNE
BROTHERS · LIMITED

206/7, HIGH STREET, EXETER—Tel. Exeter 4804

'"Quality of Utility clothes has depreciated by 50 per cent," declared Mr. H. L. Kahn, head of a London dress firm. The reason, he claims, is that wages and costs of materials have increased faster than the Utility ceiling prices.

'And so the manufacturer runs the dresses together with a minimum of cloth and trouble in order to make himself a "reasonable" profit. The result is a dress, which, as Mr. Kahn frankly stated, "costs £5, lasts only a quarter of the time it should, and will probably be unwearable when it returns from the cleaner's."'

In the General Election of February 1950, Labour won, but with their majority slashed to only five seats. Two months later, in the Budget debate, Harold Wilson told the House that there had been pressure from some quarters to end the Utility clothing scheme. But *'It is the government's intention that the Utility scheme, which is one of our greatest national assets today and a great safeguard to the housewife, should be maintained. It is the view of all of us that the benefits of the Utility production scheme should be carried forward as a permanent feature of our economy.' Again, in September, Wilson asserted: 'I want to reaffirm the resolve of the Government to maintain Utility production. So long as the government remains in office it is our intention that the advantages of the Utility scheme shall continue.'*

ALWAYS AT THE TOP
OF THE FORM —

BRASSIÈRES

A wide variety of Utility and Lux tested Non-Utility Brassieres, Suspender belts and Girdles, Obtainable from all good-class stores.

Style 104 in Peach, White, Blue and Honeydew Nylon or Cambric. Sizes 32-38. As illustrated.

insist on this seal

HOWARD WALL LIMITED, 27 HACKNEY RD., LONDON, E.2.

ABOVE A bra ad from March 1951. Many manufacturer's ads featured both utility and non-utility.

A United Nations Conference on Tariffs and Trade met at the beginning of November 1950. The Netherlands delegation challenged Britain on the question of purchase tax, declaring that, while British-made Utility goods were not liable for tax, articles of comparable quality and price imported from abroad were, giving British goods an unfair advantage.

OPPOSITE PAGE An interesting dress which appears to be for evening wear. The scalloped bodice has a very thirties feel, and the sequined or beaded belt and chiffon sleeves are very un-austerity. It was not uncommon for people to add such pieces.

RIGHT Top designers continued to work with Utility clothes, as witnessed by this Utility raincoat by Pierre Balmain, March 1951.

In mid-December the Secretary of the National Federation of Merchant Tailors told members that, owing to reduced spending power, more of the public were now purchasing Utility clothing than at any time since the introduction of the scheme.

On 23 April 1951 Harold Wilson resigned from his position in the Cabinet in protest at the introduction of charges for NHS dentures and spectacles. He was replaced by Sir Hartley Shawcross.

In May 1951, Hervey Rhodes, Parliamentary Secretary to the Board of Trade, told the House that of the total production of made-up garments in 1950, Utility comprised an estimated 85 per cent in the case of wool and animal fibre cloths, 62 per cent of rayon cloths and 55 per cent of cotton cloths. About 85 per cent of hosiery and knitwear for the home market was Utility. He ended, 'I do not expect supplies of clothing in 1951 to be markedly different from the level of consumption in 1950.'

In the following July the Government set up a committee of inquiry, chaired by Sir William Douglas, 'To review the present system of Purchase Tax affecting those classes of goods within which Utility schemes operate (i.e., cloth, garments, footwear, household and furnishing textiles, furniture and bedding) in relation to international agreements bearing on the internal taxation of imported goods'

Another General Election took place on 25 October 1951 and the Conservatives won it with a slim, but workable, majority of 17. Within days, Peter Thorneycroft was appointed President of the Board of Trade.

PIERRE BALMAIN
World-Famous Paris Designer has created a complete range of waterproofs & raincoats exclusively for Alligator RAINWEAR

"JAUNTY." Utility all wool raincoat, can be worn all-round belted, half-belted or swagger. Hood is detachable. Approximately £9.9.9

"LA LAINE." A Utility all wool raincoat with a detachable hood, in full range of Balmain colours. Approximately £9.9.0.

See the complete Alligator range now being displayed at all leading stores. Name of nearest stockist gladly sent.

ALLIGATOR RAINWEAR LTD., LONDON, W.I. & MANCHESTER

ABOVE A Utility jacket from March 1951, still retaining the three button front of earlier models.

Some hoped, while others feared, that the new Government would get rid of Utility as soon as it could. At the beginning of December the Labour MP Barbara Castle asked Thorneycroft in the Commons, '…*will he give the House a firm assurance that the rumour which is going round that the Government intend to tamper with this scheme is false, and that he will, in fact, maintain it?*' Thorneycroft only replied: '*The honourable Lady should not pay too much attention to these rumours.*'

Early in January 1952 price controls on non-Utility clothes (except for children's wear and nylons) were removed; they would now be controlled by means of cash maximum prices only. In late February the Douglas Committee proposed a new system of purchase tax, under which Utility goods would no longer enjoy automatic exemption; this received a doubtful reception. The **Dundee Courier** noted, *'First comments from furniture manufacturers and shoemakers were adverse. Drapers were readier to admit advantages in the change, although they foresaw complications in putting it into effect.'* At the end of that month, a delegation of 24 members of women's groups met Thorneycroft to discuss ways of keeping shoddy goods out of the shops if the Utility scheme ended.

Tax Increase
on FURS

With the abolition of Utility Furs and the big tax increase, all new deliveries of Furs will cost much more. Fortunately we have a comprehensive stock of fine quality Coats in practically all fashionable Furs, which we will offer AT OLD PRICES WHILE STOCK LASTS. Don't miss this unique saving opportunity. Why not inspect this collection NOW?

W. H. Scott
Manufacturing Furrier.
63 MURRAYGATE, DUNDEE.

ABOVE LEFT An advertisement from October 1952. Utility furs were no more, and purchase tax concessions had been eliminated, so furs would now 'cost much more'.

On 10 March a conference called by the National Union of Tailors and Garment Workers urged the Government to retain the Utility Clothing scheme in full. However, on the next day Parliament passed a motion removing Utility's exemption from purchase tax. One of the critical pillars of the scheme had been removed.

Two days later, addressing Parliament, Thorneycroft spoke of the Utility scheme. *'It started with a few rigid specifications from well-known manufacturers' lines introduced in times of severe shortage and linked to price control and used on a sellers' market. In those circumstances it did enable consumers to know what they were buying and ensured, or helped to ensure, that they had some kind of value for money. No one could suggest that the bulk of the old Utility scheme today provides any guarantee of value for money.*

'If anybody wishes to accuse me of murdering the old Utility scheme, I should protest that I merely have the misfortune of being caught with the body.

'I have taken the necessary steps to revoke the 118 Orders which govern the old Utility schemes and to prevent the misuse of the Utility mark after their revocation. The 1,500 or more pages of Orders and thousands of specifications will cease to have effect as from Monday next.'

ABOVE LEFT March 1951 – the original caption for this striking dress ran 'First time in Utility, a worsted georgette dress with dramatic peg-top skirt by Frank Usher at £7 11s 4d'.

ABOVE RIGHT March 1951 – 'The most dashing outfit yet in Utility! A belted suit in stone-checked tweed with matching three-quarter cape by "Travella" at £16 15s 1d.'

On 26 March the Board announced that the descriptions 'Utility' and 'non-Utility' were to be dropped when the new maximum price order came into effect on 15 April. Murdered or not, the Utility clothing scheme was dead.

Britain's Utility scheme was a unique solution to the problem of providing well-made and well-designed clothes at low cost at a time when prices were in danger of spiralling out of control. Like rationing, it was a complex scheme which depended on the kind of strict centralised regulation that could have only have happened in wartime. While effective in its day, it could not long survive peacetime in a liberal democracy. Yet in its short life it created a legend, as well as becoming one of the most recognisable and iconic symbols in Britain. This range of clothing is increasingly sought after by its many collectors, which is an eloquent testament to its importance in the social history of wartime Britain.

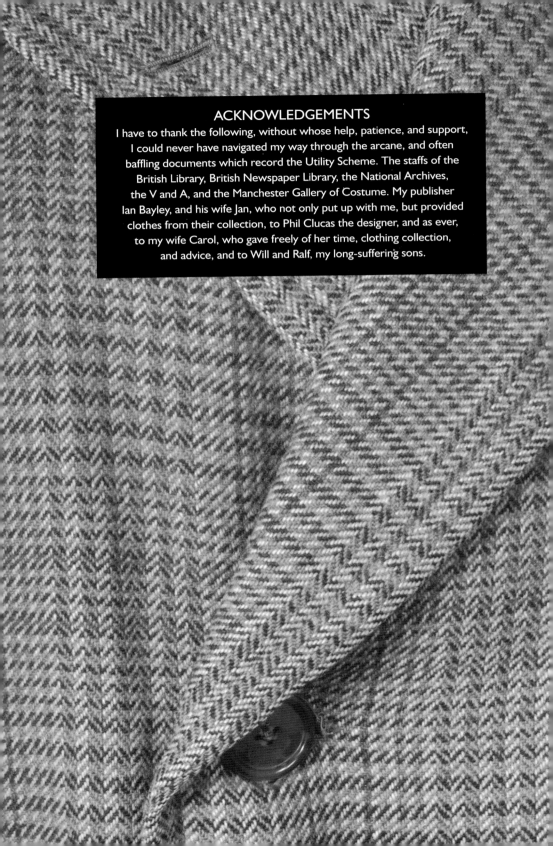

ACKNOWLEDGEMENTS

I have to thank the following, without whose help, patience, and support,
I could never have navigated my way through the arcane, and often
baffling documents which record the Utility Scheme. The staffs of the
British Library, British Newspaper Library, the National Archives,
the V and A, and the Manchester Gallery of Costume. My publisher
Ian Bayley, and his wife Jan, who not only put up with me, but provided
clothes from their collection, to Phil Clucas the designer, and as ever,
to my wife Carol, who gave freely of her time, clothing collection,
and advice, and to Will and Ralf, my long-suffering sons.